The Fall of the Imam

Nawal El Saadawi was born in the village of Kafr Tahla in Egypt. She trained as a doctor of medicine and rose to become Egypt's Director of Public Health. She began writing thirty years ago, producing novels and short stories, and in 1972 published her first study of Arab women's problems and their struggle for liberation, *Women and Sex*. She has suffered at the hands of the Egyptian censors, being forced to shift publication of her works to Beirut, and earning her dismissal from the Ministry of Health. Along with other leading Egyptian intellectuals, she was imprisoned by Sadat. She writes in Arabic, but has published several books in English, including *Woman at Point Zero*, *The Hidden Face of Eve*, *Death of an Ex-Minister* and *She Has No Place in Paradise*. Nawal El Saadawi currently lives and works in Cairo.

Sherif Hetata is a medical doctor and novelist. He is the author of six novels in Arabic, two of which have been published in English: *The Eye With an Iron Lid* (Oryx Press) and *The Net* (Zed Press). He is the husband of Nawal El Saadawi and is the translator of three of her previous works, *The Hidden Face of Eve*, *Woman at Point Zero* and *God Dies by the Nile*.

NAWAL EL SAADAWI

The Fall of the Imam

translated from the Arabic by
SHERIF HETATA

Minerva

A Minerva Paperback

THE FALL OF THE IMAM

First published in Great Britain 1988
by Methuen London
This Minerva edition published 1989
and reprinted 1989 (twice). 1990 (twice)
by Mandarin Paperbacks
Michelin House, 81 Fulham Road, London SW3 6RB

Mandarin is an imprint of the Octopus Publishing Group

Copyright © Nawal El Saadawi, 1988
Translation copyright © Methuen London 1988

A CIP catalogue record for this book
is available from the British Library

ISBN 0 7493 9003 4

Printed in Great Britain
by Cox & Wyman Ltd, Reading

To the four women I cannot forget
To Shahbani Shiraz from Iran
 Fatima Tag El Sirr from the Sudan
 Collette Itani from Lebanon
and Iitidal Mahmoud from Egypt

 For what they have suffered and
 For what they had endured.

To all the girls and boys who are still in their childhood, or
still in their youth

I dedicate this novel.

Nawal El Saadawi

Contents

Author's Preface

When I was a child, I used to see God in my dreams. He had my mother's face, the face of someone who is very just. Or he looked like my father, and then his features looked kind. My school friend Fatima Ahmed also saw God in her dreams. His face was that of her father, sometimes her uncle. It was a cruel face, the face of a person who was very unjust.

I discovered that the face of God appears to all children. Usually he looks like their mother, sometimes like their father. The problem with God's face is that neither children's eyes nor those of grown-ups can see it. God can only be seen when we sleep, and his face has the features of those who are closest to us.

I tried to write this story when I was still a young girl in school, but all my attempts were in vain. The idea was in my head, and the characters, and the impressions. Everything was so vivid! Yet I could not find the words with which to tell it. It has lived with me since then, dogged my steps. During the last ten years it has given me no respite. The characters stared at me while I was awake, and even when I slept. If I travelled inside my country, or abroad, they were always there, watching me wherever I went. They were there when I met the Iranian Shahbani Shiraz who told me the story of her 'little girl' raped by her jailers. There with Fatima Tag El Sirr, the Sudanese woman, when she took me to visit the 'Association for people with amputated hands' so that I could see her boy and his companions with their hands cut off at the wrist in accordance with Shariat*. There during the three months I spent with Iitidal Mahmoud and other young Egyptian girls in a prison cell.

* Muslim jurisprudence, which allows amputation of hands and legs for theft.

The story quivered inside me every time I caught the familiar face of one of those rulers looking out at me from a photograph, his head partly showing from under a godly turban or a military cap, or his eyes watching me in a dream as I slept. It lived with me every time I travelled to Lebanon and heard the bombs of Hizb Allah (Party of God) echoed by the bombs of Hizb El Shaitan (Party of Satan) from the other camp. It went with me to Mecca, stood by my side as I read 'Welcome to the Guests of the All Merciful' written on the wall, and behind the wall saw the man lean over the girl, put his arm around her (she was slender as a boy) and beckon to Satan. It accompanied me whenever I visited my village, Kafr Tahla, and peered in the gaunt faces of the peasant women who are my relatives. It looked out between iron bars from the faces of women serving a life sentence in Kanatir Prison for having killed a man, or from the faces of women lying in the morgue of Medical College, or on a hospital bed, or gathered around me in the Palestinian camps of Al Salt in Jordan and Borj El Barajna, or in the Canal Zone at the war front. It was there in the pinched features of children fed with irradiated milk, dying a slow death from fear of radiation or from their greater fear of light; in the fear that looked out from the faces of girls veiled in black, or the faces of people celebrating the Big Feast, or lined up for elections and plebiscites, or attending spiritualist sessions or exorcism rites, or watching the Virgin Mary descend from the sky or hearing about crosses that appear on the robes of Muslim girls when a powder is sprayed over them by Copts, or gazing at the hungry flames as they lick the dome of a church or climb up the minaret of a mosque at night.

The story was always with me. It haunted me with its characters. Yet every time I sat down to write, it would slip away from my fingers like mercury. Of all the characters, that of the Imam* was the most devious, the most elusive. He used hit and run tactics, advancing towards me only to retreat with remarkable haste. If I drew closer to him, to his personality and his traits, he would soon escape. And if I drew back, and kept aloof, he would slowly edge up. The

---

* Religious leader and ruler of the Muslims.

character of the representative of official opposition was also very tricky. At one time I had decided to eliminate him for good. But the Imam held on to him, pulling him back into the picture, fearing that in his absence there would be no 'democratic' touch.

The characters of the girls and the women were much more stable. But the name of Bint Allah* gave me a lot of anxiety and kept me awake long nights. I tried to find another name for her. Her name seemed to violate what is most sacred, to encroach on the holiest of holies. How could a girl dare to bear the sacrilegious name of Bint Allah (she also dared to bear a child without a father)? Christianity has permitted a male, Christ the Messiah, to be called the Son of God. But no one has ever heard of Bint Allah, the Daughter of God. And one day, right in the middle of the novel, she asked me a question. What if I was the Virgin Mary and had born a female child instead of a male? Would she have become Christ the Messiah?

This made it difficult for me to change the name of Bint Allah to something else. Besides, since the moment she was born until the moment she was stoned to death, people had always called her Bint Allah. Then came the day when I came upon her, a lifeless body, lying face downwards on sand and rock. I decided to banish her from my life, to forget. Things could no longer go on like this. How could I write a story in which names and events and characters forced themselves upon me all the time? It was better to give up. But when I took this decision something very strange happened. Instead of going their way, all the characters of my novel came back, abandoning themselves to me of their own free will. And as soon as I sat down again in front of my paper, they started moving over the lines, all by themselves, writing their own story out. I did not have to interfere at all with their personal or their public life, except every now and then when I was obliged to do so to prevent some of them from using words which could be considered sacrilegious, or a violation of the human values we respect. This was particularly necessary with the Imam himself. I could not allow him to exercise

* Daughter of God.

absolute power in my story, just as he had done in everything else. I said to myself, at least where my novel is concerned I should enjoy some freedom, exercise some control over the Imam, and not let him do just as he likes.

Nawal El Saadawi
Cairo, February 1987

The Search Begins

It was the night of the Big Feast. They hunted me down after chasing me all night. Something hit me in the back. I was looking for my mother in the dark, running alone with my dog following in my tracks. Something struck me from behind. I turned round to face them, but they disappeared like frightened fish. They cannot look into the sun, cannot bear its light. They sleep all day and rise up at night. They do not know how to fight, have no honour, have no pride, they always hit you from behind.

Before I fell, before letters and words had time to fade, I asked them: Why do you always let the criminal go free and punish the victim? I am young. My mother died a virgin and so will I. They said: You are the child of sin and your mother was stoned to death. But before the letters could fade from my mind, before my mind became a blank, I said: I am not the child of sin, I am Bint Allah. That's how they called me in the orphanage. Even if I lose my memory, I cannot forget. I cannot forget my mother's face. After I was born, she went to fight the enemy. She is a martyr. They said: Your mother never knew what loyalty meant, neither to our land, nor to the Imam Allah.* She died an infidel, and is burning in hell. I said: Before the life blood leaves my brain and memory ends, my mother was never a traitor. Before I was born my father abandoned her and ran away. They said: And pray who might your father be? And I said: My father is the Imam. They screamed: Not another word. May your tongue be cut out of your head.

They cut out her tongue first. Later came the rest. For the

---

* Religious leader and ruler, representative of God on earth.

Imam ruled according to the laws of God's Shariat.* Stone adulterous women to death. Cut off the hands of those who commit a theft. Slash off the tongues of those who spread rumours about irradiated milk. Pour all bottles, all casks, all barrels of alchoholic drink, into the waters of the river.

The eve of the Big Feast they slink away before the spies of the Imam can see them, descend to the river and drink from its waters until their minds are blank. In the morning, suddenly awake, they get up full of remorse, clamouring for mercy, since on the night of the Big Feast the Imam graciously pardons everyone. The doors of prisons and concentration camps are thrown open, and out of them march the dead, the martyrs, the victims of nuclear radiations, the women stoned to death, the thieves who have one foot missing on the right and one hand missing on the left.

It was her turn to be free, but the spies of the Imam spotted her as she slipped out, trying to escape in time. They saw her running in the black of night with her dog close behind her. It was just before dawn. She had almost given them the slip when something struck her in the back. As she fell, the question echoed in her mind: Why do you let the criminal go free, and kill the victim?

Their voices faded away into the silence. Her mind was dark as night, her memory all black or white, retaining not a word, not a letter from the alphabet. Only her mother's name remained behind.

* Muslim religious jurisprudence.

They Cannot Read

The darkness was impenetrable, an opaque black without sun or moon. They could not tell whether it was night, or day without daylight, in a forest thick with overgrown trees hemming them in from every side. Suddenly, from somewhere, there came a faint light, like the glimmer of a torch held in the hand of some guard, or of the Chief of Security. Just enough to catch the shadow of a body fleeing. They could tell from the running movement on two legs that it was human, not animal, not something on four legs. They could also tell it was a woman, not a man, maybe from the breasts, rounded and firm, or from something else, indefinable. She was young, very young, her bones small, her skin smooth like a child, brown as river silt, her face pointed with slanting wide-open eyes, their pupils blacker than the blackest night. A goddess of ancient times. She ran barefoot, not stopping for a moment. Her right hand carried something like the branch of a tree. Her body was naked, shining, a silver fish splitting the universe, her 'pubic shame' hidden under the wing of night, or a dark green leaf.

There was a flash of lightning, just enough for them to glimpse her disappearing into the night with the dog at her heels. Then once more everything was black and still.

A moment later something stirred in the dark, a movement made of many eyes, the eyes of the Imam advancing, led by the Chief of Security, a line of men, their huge bodies covered in hair. Each of them carried a stone or a sharp weapon in his right hand. They ran as fast as they could, trying to catch up with her, but she was light as the wind, faster than any man. Besides she knew all the secrets of the land over which she ran. This was where she had been born, and this was where she died. She would have escaped them had she not halted to fill her breast with the smell of her land.

I halted at the foot of the elevated strip of land between the river and the sea, on the way from my home to the front for the first time since we were defeated in the last war and my mother was killed. My feeling of surprise did not last but when I climbed up the slope of the hill I caught my breath in wonder. The branch in my hand slipped through my fingers, and I could feel my heart pounding. I called out my sister's name, for her time would come after me. Twenty long years; since I was born I had dreamt of this hill. I remembered every hollow, fold of the earth, pebble and stone, the feel of sea air on my body and its smell in my nose, the rise looking down on the green valley, and the three date palms and the mulberry tree. I could smell the odour of my mother's body, like fertile soil. This was my land, my land.

She would have escaped had she not been halted by the smell of the land and the sea, bringing back her whole life in one moment. She halted, took a deep breath, and just at that moment the bullet struck her in the back and bored its way through like an arrow straight to her heart. She dropped to the ground, bleeding slowly. Her dog whimpered once and was silent, and the birds flew up in fright, filling the universe with their cries. The heavens echoed with the crowing of cocks, the squawking of crows, the neighing of donkeys, and after a while the dogs joined in barking loudly. It was the end of the night, and dawn had not yet broken. Men clothed in white robes, their faces covered in thick black beards, rose up from where they lay on the ground and in great haste climbed up to the top of the minarets and domes, fixed microphones to them as fast as they could, and rapidly climbed down again leaving the electric wires dangling in the open. A thousand voices united as one voice in the call to prayer, then, resounding in the air like thunder, hailed the Imam as the 'One and Only Leader'. But right in the middle of all this commotion there was a sudden hush. The electric power had failed and the chanting voices ceased their halle-lujahs. In the deathly silence of those moments they killed

4

her. No one witnessed the crime. No one saw her drop to the ground. Only the stars in space, and the trees and the low hill rising on a stretch of land between the river and the sea. Her dead body was turned to stone, became a statue of rock living on year after year with her dog by her side (in ancient history cavemen survived with their dogs in the depths of the earth for over three hundred years).

She was a girl on her own all alone with her dog (her sisters were to follow later). The world was as it is today. Things were the same. The sky, the earth, the trees, the houses, the river, and the sea. I asked: Is this the Mediterranean Sea? And is this the River Nile? They said: Here names can be different and time passes. But the place is the same, and the sun is the same, and the ears of corn are the same, and the she-buffalo has a black skin and four legs, and I could see her in the distance descending towards the river, swimming in the water with her back shining in the sun, her eyelids drooping with pleasure as she floated lazily. After a while she climbs out of the water on to the bank, moving with a relaxed ambling gait towards the edge of a field where she stands munching fodder slowly, swinging her tail, her ears listening intently to the wheeze of the water-wheel, her brooding eyes following the woman tied to it with a rope of hemp, as she goes round and round blindfolded. A man walks behind her switching his stick over her buttocks every time she halts to take her breath. A gasp of surprise escapes my lips. A woman turning a water-wheel while the buffalo rests? They said: Here we follow the laws of offer and demand. A buffalo costs more on the market than a woman, so a man can have four wives, but he can only afford one buffalo.

I stood there surrounded by open space. The fields are like a long green ribbon, and a line of buffaloes float in the water, their backs shining in the sun. Behind the green ribbon is the desert, and behind the desert are dunes of yellow sand. But if you go as far as the hilly rise in the land you may run into bands of roaming brigands. Here hyenas and even eagles eat carrion. Tigers devour antelopes and deer but they refrain from human flesh. Men are the only living beings that feed on the flesh of their own kind. The meat of deer is rare, but

5

human beings are everywhere and their flesh is easy to find. Crocodiles are treacherous, and the skin of snakes is smooth, but their poison is deadly. Here loyalty does not exist except among dogs. It is still night. The night is long, and dark, very dark. Insects hide in its depths. They have the bodies of mosquitoes, or locusts, or rats. There are also reptiles and other beings that crawl on four legs.

But where have the people gone? I ask. I can see no one. The body of the girl has disappeared, and her assassins have left. Where have the human beings gone? I ask again. But there are millions of them, they said, like gnats floating around. You cannot see them with your eyes. They live deep in the earth, in subterranean caves, in houses like burial pits. They think that light is fire and are afraid of it. They think that the rays of the sun carry nuclear radiations, that great evil will come to them from across the ocean, dispatched by the great powers in tins of children's milk, that all this is the wrath of God descending upon them. But why should God be angry with them? They do not know. They do not know what crimes they have committed. They do not know God's word, nor what it says. God's word is written and they can neither read nor write. They do not know what words are. All they know is to murmur, or applaud, or acclaim, or vociferate, or cry out, or shriek at the top of their voices.

I asked: Is it not possible to talk to them a while? They said: Yes, if you speak their language, wear men's clothes, or hide your shameful parts behind a veil. I exclaimed in great surprise: Hide what shameful parts, since I am wearing all my clothes? Then they pointed their sharp fingers at my face. A sudden fear took hold of me and my tongue was tied. But I said: Who told you that? And they answered: God, God's words have said a woman's face is shameful and should not be seen by man or God. But God's words are written, are they not? and you do not read, so how can you know what he has said? I said. They were silent for some time. They looked at one another. They raised their eyes to heaven. They pointed to the picture hanging from the top of the monument built in commemoration of the Great Victory. I looked up and said: Who is he? They gasped: Don't you know who he is? Wherever you look you'll see him. His

6

picture hangs in every place, in the streets, on the walls, in shops, on all the arches, and columns and monuments commemorating victory. His name is the Imam and he is everywhere. But, said I, he who is everywhere is nowhere. They looked at me silently for a while. Then they pursed their lips and said: We have sworn eternal loyalty to him. He is our master, the Imam. God has visited him many a time and so he knows His word better than anyone else.

I Hear My Mother Calling

When I was a child God used to visit me while I slept. He spoke to me, in a gentle voice like my mother's. I was thinking of that when I heard the bullets being fired from a gun in quick succession, and saw the picture of the Imam fall to the ground. I started to run. Death is easy when it is quick. The head severed from the body with a sword, or a bullet in the heart. But nothing is more terrible than to die slowly. They tie me with ropes, and throw me in a pit, then hurl stones at me, one stone following another, day after day, one day following another until fifty days have passed, or a hundred, or a thousand. My body dies, but my spirit will not give up. They are worn out by so much stone-throwing, and I can see their hands hanging limply at their sides, the blood dripping from their fingers drop by drop, but my arteries are not emptied yet. My spirit inhales dust and sand, turns my body into rock, makes the stones bounce off. And I can see her in the distance, a figure carved in rock on the hill between the river and the sea. There she stands waiting in the night, ever since she gave me life, her face to the river, and her back to the sea. Twenty years have passed but there she stands upright as always. Twenty years have passed and her voice still calls to me in a soft whisper, like the rustle of the wind in the trees, or a distant call rising from the deep: Bint Allah, here. Come here.

My dog's name is Marzouk*. He has been with me since my mother brought me into the world and he stayed with me right to the end. He does not read or write. He has not read God's word, yet he is the only one who knows the truth, knows that the blood of the Imam has not soiled my hands.

* Fortunate creature of God.

8

For how can a daughter kill her father? Nobody knows that the Imam is my father, and that were it not for him, my unknown father (and for my known mother of course), I would never have been. Only my mother and my dog Marzouk know he is my father. It was Marzouk who saw my mother kneeling on the ground stifling her sobs, and it was Marzouk who saw my father slipping away in the dark. He took a good look at his face, and since then he has never forgotten. That's why every time he sees his picture hanging up, he immediately starts barking loudly. People have never been able to work out why he barks like that. They do not understand the language of dogs, whereas dogs understand the language of people. Just like human beings dogs have a memory, which registers how things develop, how events unfold themselves. They have a memory for history and Marzouk continues to remember my father the Imam when he ran away from my mother. He chased after him, bit him from behind, tore off his trousers over the left buttock, and a big piece of calico caught on to his fang. Its colour was khaki like the clothes worn by soldiers in the army, and it smelt of sweat, and cheap perfume, and other things.

The Imam was so scared of Marzouk that he ran away as fast as he could and as he ran his footsteps echoed with a metallic noise, for the heels of his shoes were fitted with iron hooves. He went on running, his eyes raised to heaven since his faith in God was great. He kept muttering: Grant me victory over my enemies, grant me that the desires of my heart come true. His bulging eyes were full of dark yearning and his lips were thick with lust for possession. He wanted a throne on earth, and a throne in heaven, a summer palace overlooking the sea, and a winter palace down south. He also wanted a palace in heaven for his after-life, deep cool rivers flowing under it, and numerous concubines both female and male. His tongue was dry and he was thirsty, but he never ceased running, his mouth open, his breath panting. Ever since childhood he had suffered a feeling of deprivation and he went through life carrying it with him. His desire to possess things was like a chronic disease, like a great hunger, and he had an unlimited faith in God's power, in what He could do for him. He developed a patch of rough blue skin

9

on his forehead from repeated prostration, and in his right hand he held a rosary of yellow beads for all to see, testimonies of his devotion to God. Over his right buttock hung a sword, encased in a long sheath and over the left buttock he held his hand hiding the hole in his trousers.

He disappeared into the night muttering words of gratitude to God, his mouth exhaling an odour of wine and of sweat from the bodies of unhappy women, and Marzouk continued to bark but nobody seemed to hear him. The coloured rockets of the Big Feast were bursting in the sky, and from a thousand microphones poured out an endless stream of words, for the Imam was speaking to his people and the speech was being broadcast on the air beginning with 'In the name of God' and ending with 'Praise be to His Holy Prophet'.

They dispersed after the speech was over, disappearing into their houses. They felt carried away with a kind of exhilaration, with a feeling of victory over some unknown foe which mounted to their heads, but in their mouths was a bitterness, a vague taste of defeat. Meanwhile the streets filled up with men carrying knives. They were all shouting the same word, repeating it time after time. Butcher. Then all of a sudden they ceased their shouting and there was a vast silence, a mysterious gloom, but the silence did not last. It was broken by screams, the piercing screams of those being sacrificed rising up from every house, followed by clouds of dense smoke heavy with the smell of burning flesh.

After eating they put on new clothes, and shoes with iron hooves fitted to the heels. Their footsteps could be heard clinking on the pavements and the streets, and their voices were raised in thanksgiving to God for His bountiful mercy. In their left hands they carried a rosary of prayer beads, and in their right hands each of them carried a stone. For the time had come and they were ready to do what had to be done. The time had come for them to stone the Devil to death.

They tied her up with hemp cord and gathered in a circle around her, vying with one another to see who could throw more stones, who could strike her more often on the bull's eye over her belly, where Satan had branded her with his

10

mark. It had been made known that he who won would be decorated with the Order of Chivalry and Honour and presented with a small palace adjoining the palace of the Imam as well as concubines to entertain him with their charms.

Under her body the earth was cool, but her nose was choked with dust. They pegged her to the ground, bared her bosom, and pulled her arms and legs apart. In her ears echoed the sound of drums, and children's laughter, and over her head floated the coloured balloons. Her eyes kept searching among the children for the face of her child. At one moment she caught a glimpse of a small wan face hemmed in by people all around, waved her hand and whispered in a voice like the rustle of tree leaves in the wind: Bint Allah, here. . . . Come here.

Ever since the moment I was born her voice has echoed in my ears, calling out to me in the rustle of the wind and the movement of leaves. Her features are part of my memory, are lines cut into its stone. I see her standing there, a statue of rock, bathed in light, the contours of her body shrouded in a dark haze. Her fingers are clasped over her heart, her features are sharp, unyielding, yet composed. She is a woman who gave her life and received nothing in return. In her eyes is the pain of discovery. The shock is over, but the sadness lingers on, like a pure light in her face, or some new vision of the world. Her body is slender, almost innocent of flesh, a spirit or a dream, unneeding of movement, or of words to be, yet with a consistency of its own palpable beneath an envelope of air. Her head is held upright and she smiles the smile of a woman who has lost everything and kept her own soul, has unveiled the secrets of the world, and pierced through the mask of heaven. Her suffering shows in the furrows of her face, so deep that they have grooved themselves into the bone, but her eyes continue to shine with an inner glow.

The guardian shut the last door in the palace of the Imam, repeating the verse of the Seat under his breath to ensure that all devils and djinns were shut out. Everyone slept: the Imam, his spies, the devils, the angels, the gods. Even the trees and

11

the wind slept. She alone remained awake, her eyes wide open, her body upright, standing for a long time without the slightest movement, her arms holding something tightly pressed against her. She looked around cautiously, bent down until her head almost touched the ground, and started to smooth it out with her peasant's hand, brushing aside the stones and pebbles. Then she covered the surface with earth to make it soft like a mother's lap, quickly wrenched me away from her breast with her hands and laid me down on my bed.

There I lay fast asleep. My face peering out of an opening in the white wrappings was a pale patch in the night and my chest rose and fell with the deep breathing of a child. One of my hands crept out of its sleeve, palm upwards to the sky as though soliciting the mercy of the powers on high.

She took off her black woollen shawl and wrapped it carefully around me. My hand touched her finger and quickly curled around it, holding tight, refusing to let go. She abandoned it to my tiny grasp, left it to stay there for a moment as long as the endless night, as long as a mother's sigh when she leaves her child behind. Then she started to withdraw it very slowly, as though she was draining the life blood from my heart little by little. The moment her flesh parted from my flesh, I shivered and woke up. I saw her standing upright looking down at me, her face in the sky, and her eyes like stars. Then she turned round and walked away. I saw her from the back straight as a spear, walking with a long stride, neither fast nor slow, her arms swinging free as the air. The distance between us kept growing but her body seemed no smaller. It moved further and further away without changing until all at once she was gone.

The Children of God

I heard the sound of bullets being fired from a gun one after another in quick succession. I saw him fall, and as he fell I watched the face before me change slowly into another face, into a face I had never seen before, a strange face neither human nor animal, a face that belonged not to a man, or to a father, or to an Imam. It was one of those terrible faces remembered from my childhood nightmares or from the tales told to me by an old grandmother who suckled me with breast milk and stories about devils and djinns. Like all the other children in the home, I had never seen my real grandmother. We knew nothing about our fathers, or our mothers, or our grandmothers. We were called the children of God, and I was called Bint Allah, the Daughter of God. I had never seen God face to face, yet I thought He was my father, and that my mother was his wife.

In my sleep I often used to dream of my mother. She stands in an open space waiting for God. The night is dark and everyone has gone to bed, but there she is standing alone, in the same place where I always find her. I am lying on the ground and can see her face high up above me cut out against the sky. Her eyes shine with light and her voice reaches me like a whisper carried by the wind. I hear her call out softly: Bint Allah, come here. I get out of bed and walk on my bare feet towards the voice. It reaches me from a distance, sounding muffled as though separated from me by a door. I open the door and look out. There is no one. I walk down a long corridor and still there is no one. At the end is another door but nearby I discover an open window, which looks out on to a courtyard. I jump up to the window-sill in one leap, slip out and walk along the edge of a wall. I hold out my arms in front of me. My body keeps its balance well and

13

I do not falter, moving as easily and as swiftly as a feather. My feet scarcely touch the ground for I am like a spirit without a body. At the end of the wall I jump off into the courtyard, landing on all fours like a cat, crouching silently without moving, straining my ears to catch any sound in the dark. Little by little I begin to hear something like whispers coming from behind a closed door. The door is made of wood and is painted a bright green like a field of young wheat. Light filters through a crack in the wood.

Who stands there in the dark?

It's me.

Who are you?

Bint Allah.

Come here, Bint Allah.

I enter a small room. It is almost dark inside. Behind the door stands a woman, the wife of the guard. She is dressed in a black robe which is wide around her body and wears a white kerchief knotted over her head. She stretches out her hands to me. They are brown as earth and her eyes shine like stars in the night. Her chest heaves up and down with a sobbing breath. Her skin is smooth and her breasts are full of milk. I can see her hold the dark erect nipple between her fingers and squeeze the pain out of it drop by drop, like tiny pearls of milk or sap oozing from dry bark. The small crib beside her is empty and on the other side her husband sleeps on snoring loudly. His face is webbed in wrinkles and his dark beard is rolled up over his chin under a thin worn blanket. He opens his eyes suddenly and stares at me as I nestle in her arms. I can see his bloodshot eyes fix themselves for a long moment on my face before he shouts out in a loud voice: This is not my child. Whose child is she? The woman answers: She is Bint Allah. He lifts his hand high up in the air and brings it down on her face with all his might. You adulterous whore. You daughter of an adulterous bitch, he screams.

I open my eyes in the dark. In the beds I see rows of children lifting their heads to look around. Near my bed lies a girl of my age whose name is Nemat Allah.* I call her sister. She

* Blessing or gift of God.

14

has black silky hair and it lies on her pillow above the bed cover. Her eyes are wide open and she gasps with silent sobs. Then the gasping stops and I can hear her whisper softly: Bint Allah, come here.

I get out of bed and lie down beside her. She winds her arms around me, and her body starts to shake again. I am afraid, she says. Afraid of what? I am afraid of God. Why? I do not know. Are you not afraid of God? I am Bint Allah, the Daughter of God, so why should I be afraid of Him? Why should I be afraid of my father? She holds me tight and I can hear her heart beat. Her bosom is round and smooth like a mother and we sleep in each other's arms until dawn. Before sunrise she wakes me up: Bint Allah, go back to your bed. Orders in the home were strict. A bell rings when it is time to sleep and no one is allowed to leave their bed. If two children are caught together the punishment is severe. At the back of the courtyard is a punishment cell and terrible stories are told about what happens there. In front of the door stands a big tall man. His bald head shines in the light, his broad face is covered in hair and he has narrow deep-set eyes. In his right hand he holds a long stick, and in his left hand he fingers a rosary of yellow beads.

At night my sister wraps her arms around me. She weeps silently for a long time, then stifling her sobs and wiping her tears with the back of her hand, she begins to speak. She tells me how God visited her mother in a dream and how after that she became pregnant with child like the Virgin Mary. When her belly grew big she put on a wide flowing robe in order to hide what had happened. One night when everyone was fast asleep she gave birth to her child, but the eyes of the Imam always wide awake saw everything. They took her away, tied her with a rope of hemp, put her in an open space and started to stone her to death, one stone after the other without haste until she died. I held Nemat Allah tight in my arms. After a little while I said: But if God was the cause, why did they stone your mother to death? She did not know what to answer and was silent. I kept wondering about all this but was overcome by sleep and so my questions remained unanswered. No sooner had I fallen asleep than I started to dream.

15

In the dream I see God in the form of a man. He stands in front of a door with his right hand hidden behind his back. His face is covered with hair but his head has no hair at all and it shines in the light. I keep my eyes tightly closed and my body shivers under the bed covers. The man moves his hand out from behind his back, raises it up in the air in front of my eyes and opens his fingers, showing me that he carries no stick. His voice is gentle when he speaks, Bint Allah, come here. I can feel his hand touch me. It is big and caressing, and the palm has the feel of a mother's bosom. I lay my head on his chest and shut my eyes, as he caresses my face. Slowly his hand moves down to my breasts, then to my belly. My body is traversed with a strange spasm, like a deep shaking from within. I can hear his voice whisper in my ears: Don't be afraid, Bint Allah. I am God and you will give birth to your son the Christ.

I wake up suddenly, shaking with fright. It is still dark. My body is bathed in sweat, smells of God, of holiness. My hand moves down, feeling its way over my swollen belly. Something moves inside me and under my hand I can feel a pulse beating in unison with my heart. The night is black and dawn has not yet started to break through. Slowly a faint light starts to creep through the shutters and above my head the high ceiling is turning grey. I can see the lampshade hanging down from it at the end of a long wire. The wire is black with flies and the flies are fast asleep. The children have not awakened yet and their heads are jutting out from under the bedcovers like black insects. Near me Nemat Allah is asleep and her long tresses hide her face with a mask of black silk. I close my eyes, trying to fall asleep again, but the holy smell of God lingers in my nose, and his voice echoes in my ears like a soft whispering. He hides his hand behind his back, but I no longer fear him. I know he does not carry a stick, and that his hand is as gentle and caressing as the hand of my mother. He moves up closer to me, advancing with a slow step. I see his face appearing under the light, but it is no longer the same face as it was before. Now the eyes are red and burn with a fierce light. He stretches out his long arm towards me and I can feel the iron grasp of his thick fingers around my neck. I try to wrench myself free and run but my body seems tied to the ground. I open my mouth to call out to my mother but there is no sound, as though my voice is paralysed. Suddenly there is a tremendous noise. It reverberates in my ear drums, and shakes the heavens above. I am seized with fright wondering what it can be. Rockets shooting to the sky in celebration of the Big Feast? Voices raised in a great hallelujah? Or . . . people screaming?

The Old Face of Baba

It was a noise like the sound of shots fired from a gun in quick succession. The body of the Imam collapsed before my eyes but his face remained suspended in the sky all lit up like the sun. Then a sound of thunder echoed in the air and suddenly there was no light, only nuclear radiation. The face of the Imam slowly bowed towards the earth, becoming darker and darker until it could no longer be distinguished from the ground on which it came to rest. Everything happened within the space of seconds, yet time slowed down from the moment he stood on the platform with his face lit up like that of God in heaven, until he collapsed with a face as livid as the Devil. I had never met the Devil in person, and could only remember what he looked like in my dreams or in the stories told by the old grandmother in the orphanage. We used to gather around her in a circle and listen to her tales about devils and djinns until a bell rang ordering us to bed. Those were the days in the children's home when I knew neither my mother nor my father. But in my sleep I used to see God come and go. He had two faces, one smooth and gentle like the bosom of my mother, and the other covered in hair and rather fierce looking. He always appeared in the form of a man whom the children called Baba.

Baba was the first man I ever saw in my life. All of a sudden we would find him standing in front of us, and the next moment, just as suddenly, he would disappear. I never saw him coming in or going out through the door. He would be there, standing with his legs straddled apart in the middle of the courtyard like someone who has risen through a hole in the earth or fallen from the sky. He had a big beard and his face was covered with hair. It had a fixed expression as though its muscles never moved. Yet his head was bald and

18

the skin over it shone every time the sunlight fell where he stood. His white shirt remained wide open at the neck, allowing the black bristly hair covering his chest to protrude. He had a broad chest with big rib bones and his breast muscles were always powerfully tensed, leaving no place for soft flesh under the skin. Over each breast was a nipple, all black and rough and shrivelled like some old ugly fruit showing under the thin tissue of his shirt. Around his waist he wore a broad belt fastened so tightly that it pushed his belly up against the muscles of his back. His small buttocks looked hard under the stretched leather of his pants, and his bow legs stood out prominently below the knees, but his thighs were narrow like those of a tiger, rising upwards to meet under the belly over a small lemon-like swelling hanging down in between.

His right hand always held a stick while his left was closed most of the time around the arm of some small girl he was dragging off to the punishment cell. After shutting the door on her, he would return to the courtyard, sit on a cane chair and call out to the children. We gathered around him, sitting in a circle on wooden benches and the lesson on religious catechism would begin. He recited in a slow, throaty voice, holding the stick in one hand and the Holy Book of God in the other. Say I seek refuge in the Lord of the Breaking Day. From the Mischief of Things Created. From the Mischief of Darkness when it Envelops. From the Mischief of Those Blowing into the Embers of Occult Magic. After a while my eyes close and I go to sleep. I dream of those who blow into the embers of Occult Magic. They are black eagles hovering in the sky over my head. I awaken to his voice as he roars: What is the punishment for theft? And the children answer in one breath: Cutting off the hand. What is the punishment for adultery? They shout back in chorus: Stoning until death. Then everything is silent. We can hear each other breathing. Nemat Allah is beside me on the bench. I can see her staring at me with eyes big enough to contain all the fear in the world. She whispers: What is adultery? I close my eyes and hold my breath trying to escape back into sleep but am awakened again as he roars. Say He is God, the One and Only, God the Absolute, the Eternal. He begetteth not, nor

19

was He begotten, and there is none like . . . . Nemat Allah huddles close up to me and rests her head against my cheek. Under her breath she whispers again: Did not God beget the Lord Christ?

Her voice could scarcely be heard, for it was no higher than the expiration of her chest, but his deep-set eyes switched over to us quickly and he shouted loudly: Someone spoke. Who is it? Now no sound could be heard except the whirl of his stick cutting through the air again and again. Before my eyes I could see the sacrificial lamb tied by one of its forelegs as it tried desperately to free itself, bleating all the time. The children were stealing quick looks at the animal straining furiously at the rope but their ears carefully followed the sound of Baba's hoarse voice as he related the story of Abraham. And while they slept God's voice spoke to the father, ordering him to sacrifice his son, and when the father awoke he seized hold of his son, and laid a knife against his throat.

The children kept huddling closer and closer to one another, as though each of them was trying to hide by slipping into the body of the other. The long stick moved out over their heads, shining like a knife, and came to rest on Fadl Allah's* neck. He was sitting near me, curled up around himself like a child in its mother's womb. His fingers blue with cold sought refuge in my hand and his bare knee rested on the bench close to mine. He kept pulling at the edge of his long robe made of calico trying to prevent the icy current of air from reaching under it. His face was pale, almost bloodless, and the wooden bench swayed under him with a squeaky noise like grinding teeth. I clasped his hand in mine and in a voice as low as possible asked him: But what wrong did the son commit so as to make his father think of killing him? But Baba heard me, for he could hear what we said even before we had time to say it, and he could see what we did even though we did not notice him watching us. He shouted in a loud voice: A father can question his son, but on no account can a son question his father. To

* God's bounty.

20

obey God is an unbreakable law and without obedience to father and husband there can be no obedience to God.

He lifted the stick from where it still lay on Fadl Allah's neck and pointed in the direction of the lamb tied to a peg. He said: This lamb will be sacrificed on the occasion of the Big Feast. We will eat its meat. Our Lord Abraham obeyed the will of God. Ishmael obeyed the will of his father. And so now it is the animal which is sacrificed. With this sentence the lesson on religious catechism came to an end. A moment later Baba had disappeared from the courtyard. But Fadl Allah remained seated on the bench unable to move his legs, his head resting on his knees as though he was plunged in deep thought.

The bell rang summoning the children to bed. I got up from the bench followed by Fadl Allah. His long robe was wet at the back and clung to his body over his legs. Where he had sat there was a small pool of water which I swept away with the palm of my hand before anyone could notice it. There was a strong smell of urine on my hand. I dried it quickly on my clothes and ran off to the latrines. Through the window I could see the punishment cell at some distance in the middle of the courtyard and, behind, the dome of the church and the minaret of the mosque. It lay hidden under the shade of a huge tree, surrounded by something like a dark haze so that its walls were almost invisible, bathed in an atmosphere of obscure, almost holy mystery. Its door was made of wood painted yellow with a metal doorknob and on the doorknob were old dried stains like blood.

My eyes were fixed on the doorknob. It did not move, nor did the door open to let Nemat Allah out. I closed my eyes and slept, then after a while woke up. The door was still closed. By my side I found Fadl Allah and when I looked at him he pulled something out from under his long robe. It was a loaf of bread, and the smell of fresh baking went to my head. I had not eaten since the morning lesson, so we ate, then we lay on a window-sill with our arms around each other. My long robe had a strong smell of urine about it, and Nemat Allah was still locked up in the cell. I said to myself, when I grow up I will kill him.

It seemed he could hear everything we said, for just at that

21

moment he appeared in front of us as though his big body had broken through the layers of the earth to reach its surface. The muscles of his face were contracted, and the tangled hair protruded through his open shirt. Under it the breast muscles were tense and the two dark nipples stood out almost erect. He stared at us fixedly as we lay in one another's arms on the window-sill. I could see his nostrils tremble as though he was following a scent and their openings grew wider, exposing their dark pits.

My turn had come to be punished. I had been expecting it every day like a dark fate that hung over my head. I felt his thick fingers close tightly over my arm. I closed my eyes and abandoned myself. He was God, and he could take me wherever he wished. I woke from my sleep to find myself lying in bed. There was a feeling of wetness under my body, and over my thigh was something warm and sticky like sweat. I moved my hand towards it wondering what it could be, touched my thigh and then drew it slowly out from under the covers. I held it up in front of my eyes. My finger tips were covered in blood.

Only Once in History

As I ran with Marzouk following closely in my wake, the bullet hit me in the back. Before I lost all trace of what had happened, before my mind went black, I made an effort to remember, to record the history of events and retain some sequence of the alphabet. I was fully dressed. They were pointing at my face, which they called my shameful part. I recall how my body rebelled despite the threat of death. I said: Who told you that? It is God's word, they said. But, said I, His word is written and you neither read nor write. So who told you that? They remained silent for a while. They looked at one another, lifted their eyes to heaven, pointed to the picture which was hanging on the monument to victory. They said: It is our Lord the Imam who has seen God and knows His word. So I asked: Where did the Imam see God? They said: God visited him while he slept. I made an effort to remember before all memory of things is dead. But God also visited me in my sleep, I said. God does not visit women nor does He reveal himself to them. God visited the Virgin Mary and she was a woman, said I. They looked at me and said: That only happened once in history and God Almighty is too great to do what He does a second time. God visited the Prophet Mohamed and revealed Himself to him in visions several times, and before that He visited Abraham, so why should He repeat the same thing with the Imam? said I. They were silent for a long time. They looked at one another, lifted their eyes to the picture hanging from above. They said: He has seen God many times, but God has never revealed Himself to us.

The Chief of Security

The world was so dark that it seemed as though the sun had been extinguished for all time. She continued to run as fast as she could, trying to get away before she was surrounded. Her dog followed behind her, his paws raising a cloud of dust. The eyes of the Imam fastened their sights on the trail of dust, following close on her tracks, with their dogs bringing up the rear, yapping and barking at their heels without a stop. At a certain moment the Chief of Security came to a halt, pulled a pure silk handkerchief from out of his pocket, wiped his eyes, and then carefully polished the lenses of his glasses. Since he had been promoted to his new post he had taken to wearing dark glasses. This way he felt more secure, more satisfied, in a way superior to others. For now when he spied no one could follow his eyes as they lingered slowly on a pair of rounded thighs, or watched a child urinate in the night, or tried to pierce the disguise of the Imam slipping out of a prostitutes' house.

He was the Chief of Security and his sacred duty was to ensure that the Imam was well protected from enemies and friends alike and that the members of Hizb Allah* flourished at all times. He always sat in the front row on the right of the Imam, pressed so close up against him that he would have occupied his seat were it not for the fact that the Imam sat squarely on it. On the left of the Imam was the Great Writer, his fountain pen jutting over the edge of his pocket, his right eye fixed on the Imam in a steady unwavering gaze, his left eye straying all the time to the balcony reserved for the women of the Imam's harem. Next to him was the Leader of the Official Opposition, while in the second row behind

* Party of God.

him sat the Ministers of State, their shoulders touching, their knees pressed tightly together, their right hands held over their left breasts as though they were all seized with the fear of a common foe. The foreign guests stood in silence, a superior far-away look in their eyes, their faces and their shoes shining in the sun, their women huddled together nearby on the balcony reserved for the harem. Here also were gathered the wives of all the important personalities of state, and in their midst the Official Wife of the Imam wearing her angel's face and the Order of Highest Honour, its bright colours flowing over her rounded breast.

The Chief of Security threw one of his sidelong glances at the Official Wife. It lasted long enough for him to catch the passionate looks she was directing at the Great Writer and to notice the flicker in his eyes expressing a message of eternal devotion. The Imam however had his eyes fastened on the heavens for he believed that God was his best support in these times of political upheaval and economic crisis. The Leader of the Official Opposition seemed to be undecided. While his right eye gazed fixedly at the throne on which the Imam was seated, his left eye kept a careful watch on the Chief of Security. Every now and then the two men would exchange a smile, for this was the only thing they exchanged in broad daylight. After dark they spent many a night together drinking toast after toast to loyalty and friendship. They were great friends and bitter enemies, the Chief of Security a member of Hizb Allah, the Leader of the Opposition a member of Hizb Al Shaitan*, both parties legalized and blessed by the Imam. They were like rivals united by their common love for the same woman, and by their common and bitter hatred for one another, like step-brothers with the same mother and two fathers, united by a common hatred and a common love for the same woman.

I was standing in the first row. The air resounded with the acclamations of the crowd, and the guns being fixed in celebration of the Big Feast. The Imam had his eyes fired on the clear blue sky above him but my eyes kept roving behind my dark glasses, watching every flutter in the crowd, every

* Party of Satan.

25

flicker in a million eyes, seeing intention when movement was still a stillness in disguise, a hand preparing to be raised in defiance, a finger on a trigger touching lightly just before it tightens. I knew them one by one, knew their faces well, could see their heads slip between a thousand heads. Whether they were men or women, their features were there in my files. I glimpsed her in the crowd, right at the back, hiding her face behind a pair of shoulders and a head. I knew who she was at once without the slightest hesitation, without a need to think. Her face was thin, her features worn, exactly like her mother, bitching daughter of a bitching mother always moving underground, creeping in the dark, conspiring with outlawed movements and secret parties. A wretched woman possessing nothing but a body to be sold for the price of a meal.

I went to her once, but I was still a youth at the time and she was a young girl, almost a child. Before I could begin the first round she said to me: Show me the colour of your money. I said: Don't you trust me? You are the type who would live off a woman's sweat, she said. I was tongue-tied. How had this child been able to see through me so easily? How had the secrets of life been revealed to her? I took out my money and put it in the drawer next to her bed. Then I mounted her once, twice, thrice, any number of times, until she was exhausted and fell asleep. I opened the drawer, took out all the money I found there, put it in my pocket and tiptoed out so as not to awaken her. And year after year I continued to collect money from here and there until I had enough to build a three-storeyed redbrick house.

Then I married the daughter of a State Minister and became a member of Hizb Allah. I did not catch even a passing glimpse of her before we married. She was a very chaste woman, wore a veil and never showed herself before men. I married her in full accordance with the holy writ of God and His Prophet, and her father warranted for her in all ways. I paid a big dowry to betroth her, and we celebrated our wedding in the presence of all the notables. The Imam attended in person. But on the night of our wedding the bridal sheets remained as white as buffalo milk, with not the slightest drop of virginal blood, and I said to myself, Some-

26

body must have taken her before I did but God will compensate me for my loss. The honour of the Minister is more important than my honour and should be given precedence. Besides, God is all merciful and forgiving and I cannot pretend to place myself above Him.

I beat her until she confessed, then I forgave her just as God does with His creatures when they sin. I became her God. She worshipped me, chose to be at my feet like a dog, and now I possessed her completely but she had no hold over me at all. The more I turned away from her, the greater her passion for me grew, but I only desired those women who refused me. Each time I was refused, I remembered how my mother used to say to my father: Thou art my shadow on this earth, when I runneth away from thee thou turneth around at once and followeth me. And how the Imam was wont to say that my mind thinks only of those who oppose me without my authorization. Then I noticed his look swing towards the place in which she stood at the back of the crowd, saw her eyes shine defiantly, but when I looked at him his pupils were aflame with desire. I said to myself, this girl and no one else will be your death, for in history many a great king has met his end at the hands of a whoring woman.

The Legal Wife

The voices shouting to the heavens, God be with you, were like music to her ears. Her diamond earrings trembled to the sound, shivering with the thousand lights focussed on the Imam from all around. Her neck a slender column of the whitest marble surrounded by five rows of the purest pearl swayed ever so slightly. Over her breast she wore the ribbon of the Order and the Medal in the form of a brooch like a sun-disc radiating rays of light. On her fingers were rings and precious stones shining like stars. There she stood on the balcony reserved for the harem, surrounded by the wives of important state dignitaries, their faces mask-like, stretched in a fixed expression suited to the occasion, their silky dresses billowing over their rounded lines, their shameful parts covered by veils of the best and most expensive imported types. She stood proudly, straining her neck as far as she could to follow her husband the Imam in his slightest movement, while he in turn strained his neck as far as he could towards the throne of God, high up in the heavens, trying not to lose sight of Him even for the fraction of a second.

Her heart beat strongly under the ribs, and just below her breast cut into the white skin was a cross with Jesus nailed to it. She raised her hand, made the sign of the Trinity, stopping a moment for each of the Father, the Son and the Holy Ghost. Protect him from his enemies, Holy Mother of Christ, then adding quickly as though she had forgotten: Say O Allah that I am forgiven and that thou wilt protect him from his mortal enemies. Give him thy protection O Prophet of Allah. Did I not abandon everything for his love? Did I not abandon the Lord Christ, give up my name, my father's name, my country and even my faith? Indeed I threw away everything for him, for I was tired of washing up endless piles of plates, of breathing in the air that thousands of people had breathed in and breathed out before me in the underground tunnels where the trains came and went. I was tired of smiling into faces that never smiled, tired of going to church every Sunday and praying to God to save me from my plight. Twenty years of prayer to the Father, the Son and the Holy Ghost, and yet not one of them stretched out a helping hand.

Then came the Imam. It was he that took me away from my misery. I saw him seated on his throne and fell in love with him immediately. He carried me away in his arms and from that moment I could look proudly up into the sky. I discovered Paradise on earth and learnt to have faith in Allah and His Prophet, for now I had gardens and parks, palaces and banquet halls, servants and courtiers, rivers flowing with wine and honey, things without end from which I could choose at will. When I raised my head to look around all heads were lowered to the ground. All faces smiled at me but I did not have to smile. I walked with a serene step in front of Ministers of State amidst flashing lights to inaugurate charity bazaars and hospitals and homes. My name was now etched into the marble stones of history, was flashed on to a million screens, broadcast on the waves of sound. I was the wife of the Imam, no one was my equal, no one could occupy my place. No woman had my beauty, or my brains, or my fame.

God is with you. The acclamations continued to echo in her ears. She looked at him as he stood on the platform looking the other way. Cannons kept firing salvoes to victory and each time she heard them thunder out her heartbeat. She watched the rocket-carriers parading close in front of him and the elongated cone-shaped heads pointed to the sky above him, yet his head, the head of the one and only Imam, leader of the faithful, was covered only in a knitted skull cap, and his chest was exposed under his fine robe without protection, without the bullet-proof vest he should have worn. There he was up there on the platform, exposed with nothing to protect him except Allah and his Prophet. O Mary Mother of God take care of him and shield him from all evil. Remembering, she quickly swallowed the words and just as quickly murmured a prayer asking for forgiveness, her tongue repeating Allah's name and that of His Prophet, while her heart continued to remember the Christ. Protect him from his enemies O God. Protect him from the envy of men and women, from those that blow on the embers of Occult Magic. First amongst them is his first wife who is hiding in the crowd right at the back. Around her neck is a folded amulet hanging from a leather thong and her lips pray to God that he be transformed into a monkey and dragged around on a chain. Protect him O God from the scheming of women, for their capacity to do evil is without limit. Then O God do not forget that illegitimate daughter of his. Ever since she was born she has thought of nothing else except how to revenge herself on him. There she goes bending low behind the backs of the people in the crowd, trying to hide herself as she approaches. In her right hand she carries something long and pointed like an instrument of death.

With every new burst of acclamations, the beats of her heart vibrate in her ears. She strains herself to hear the sudden sound. What is it? Bullets fired from a gun? Her eyes blue as the sea open wide in amazement as his face drops from its place high up in the sky down to the ground. She sees other faces disappear just as suddenly from around him, and the particles of dust floating up in the air to form a fine cloud. She rubs her eyes as though awakening from deep sleep only to find that she has been awake all the time. No she was not asleep. But now she is no longer seated. She no longer feels the throne underneath her, holding her body up. Where is the throne? It has disappeared. It lies face downwards with its four legs upright in the air. She quickly draws the sign of the cross in front of her breast. What has happened O Virgin Mother Mary? The image of her mother's face is round and radiant like the sun. The Mother, the Son and the Holy Ghost, then quickly remembering, O God have mercy on me, the Father, the Son and the Holy Ghost.

Allah is on the Side of the Imam

I heard the sound of gunshots ringing in my ears. My eyes were looking upwards to the kingdom of heaven and for no more than a second I lost sight of the kingdom of earth, but it was enough. He took advantage of this short moment of inattention on my part and pulled the trigger. I did not see his face and could not tell with any certainty who he was. Perhaps one of those members of Hizb Al Shaitan whose faces I know one by one. I know their leader very well. Nobody had heard of him until I brought him out of the dark into the light, gave him a name and made him to exist. Before that he was nothing. I ordered him to become the Leader of the Official Opposition. I said to him: You can oppose all orders except mine, criticize all decrees except those issued personally by me. I alone rule this land and there is no one else besides me to decide. You shall be given a palace in Liberty Square, a monthly allowance, a daily newspaper and a seat in the Advisory Council and in Parliament.

I saw his face light up with a radiant smile. When we were young we went to the same school. He used to close his eyes and dream of seeing his picture on the front page of the newspaper. And every day he kept repeating this same dream. I also used to dream of seeing my picture on the front page, but the front pages of the newspapers only showed pictures of the heads of state, or leaders of parties, or killers of both sexes, or famous whores. At school he sat next to me. His trousers were made of expensive wool whereas my trousers always had a hole over the seat and I had to keep my hand behind my back to hide it. My father was a poor peasant and hoped I would grow up to be one of the guards in the palace of the Imam. But his father was rich, had travelled overseas

31

to complete his education, had learnt to speak foreign languages and wore the clothes of city people. He married a woman who believed in Christ and could not converse in Arabic. She had fair hair and the skin of her legs was so white and so transparent that without touching her one could almost feel the warmth of the flesh under it. She was like one of those beautiful maidens reserved for the believers in Paradise. My eyes used to follow her with the hunger of someone who had never known what it was like to be with a woman. There had been many women in my life, but poverty had continued to stick to me like my skin, and this woman was so different from the others I had met. To this day I have never been able to rid myself of my fear of poverty and hunger. No matter how much I ate there was always this hunger gnawing at me deep inside. And no matter what I did in order to feel secure, my mind was never at rest. Each day I saw my picture in the newspapers or hanging up everywhere flooded with light. Each day I closed my eyes and dreamt the old dream where I saw myself seated on two thrones, the throne of earth and the throne of heaven.

Ever since my childhood whenever I slept Allah visited me in my dreams. His face was my father's face, the features covered in a web of wrinkles, the skin pitted by smallpox. Over his right pupil was a small white scar, the remains of an early inflammation, of pus in his eyes. He wore the long peasant robe and a woollen skull cap frayed thin at the edges by daily use. In the dream He called out to me in my father's loud voice, addressing me as thou, Imam. I answered meekly: I am at thy beck and call Allah. He said: I shall bestow upon thee what thou desirest and it shall be without limits whether on earth or in the heavens, but on one condition. And what could that be my Lord? said I. He stretched out His arm towards me and I could see that in His hand he held something. It was a rosary of yellow beads dangling down between His fingers, and the skin over His fingers was brown and coarse and cracked just like the fingers of my father. This rosary has thirty-three beads, said He. If you make it to circle through your fingers three times it will give the number of ninety-nine, and with each bead you are to repeat one of my ninety-nine names. That is my will to you, and if anybody dares to disobey you, use this. And He pulled out a long shining sword from its sheath, and brought its point up to my chest so close that it almost went through my ribs. I took a quick step backwards, and woke up, my eyes wide open with fear. My mother noticed that I was deeply shaken by something and that my face had gone very pale all of a sudden. She said: What is wrong my son? Your face is no longer your face. I have seen God, said I. But God is good and beautiful, so why are you shaking like that? He carried a sword with him and pointed it at my chest so closely that it almost went through my ribs. She spat into the neck of her long black robe and said: That is not God. It must have been the Devil whom you saw. Go, do your ablutions and pray to God that He have mercy on you.

My mother used to pray at dawn before she went to the field and then again at night when she came back. But I never saw my father kneel in prayer even once. During the fasting month of Ramadan he would eat and drink and smoke his water tobacco-pipe and divide his nights between his four wives unequally, spending three nights with his most recent wife to every night he spent with my mother. He would say: God forgives all sins no matter how great except the sin of believing in another God besides Him. For there is only one God in heaven and that is Allah, and there is only one ruler on the earth and that is the Imam.

Before he died my father paid a visit to the tomb of the Prophet in Mecca. When he came back he began to wear a cloak instead of the usual peasant attire and I used to hear him say that the pilgrimage to the Prophet's tomb washed all sins away, leaving no trace behind, no matter how oft they had been repeated. Thus it was that my father was able to die in peace without a sin on his conscience. So when my mother grew old I asked her why she had not thought of paying a visit to the Prophet's tomb before she died and so make sure that in the after-life she could join my father in Paradise. But she looked at me with weeping eyes and said: Your father sold the crops before he died and left nothing behind for me so I have no money to buy a ticket to Mecca. And as she had no way of washing away her sins, she dried her eyes on the palm of her hand and said: If Allah opens the doors of prosperity to you my son, promise to buy me a ticket so that I can go to the Prophet's tomb. I promise to do that for you mother, said I. But the days went by and I forgot all about what had passed between us. I even forgot what her face looked like, seeing all the things I had to attend to in my life. And this went on year after year until twenty years passed by without my going to see her where she lived in the same small house way up in the South. My eyes were always fastened on the heavens so that all I could see was Allah and Hizb Allah. I even forgot the existence of another party, of Hizb Al Shaitan.

In fact Hizb Al Shaitan would never have existed if I had not decreed that the creation of such a party was necessary. I said to myself, If Satan does not come and go freely among my people how are they going to know fear? And without fear, no ruler, no Imam, can remain on the throne. Hizb Al Shaitan will be there to constitute the opposition in the Advisory Council and the People's Assembly. It will say no in front of my people and whisper yes in my ear. Then I remembered my friend, for he was just the man I needed to play this role. He had inherited land and money from his father and what he was looking for now was fame, a place in history so that people would remember his name. Besides, now he had visited the tomb of the Prophet in Mecca and acquired the respected title of Haj, he was even better prepared to play this role. I of course know that his heart is empty of faith and that his wife does not believe in one God but in three, that she makes the sign of the cross and kneels to the Trinity, to the Father, the Son and the Holy Ghost. But she is blonde, like honey, slender like the fine branch of a tree, and she speaks seven tongues. He shows her off proudly in front of people and seats her beside him at state functions.

I hide my wife behind a veil and make her walk behind me in the streets. She does not know how to write her name, and she cannot read the word of God. Her mind has little substance but her body is full of flesh, her buttocks are heavy and her brain lightweight. God created her out of a gnarled and twisted rib. She was destined to be poor, to be without lineage or family, a woman of low descent. When I married

34

her God had not opened the doors of prosperity to me and we were bound together in holy poverty, but after I had risen so high and sat on the throne she was no longer a suitable wife for me, she no longer fitted in with this new stage in my life. Besides, the Advisory Council told me that the Imam has the right to a new house, a new cloak of the best material and a new wife, to a woman blonde as honey, with eyes blue as the sea and a tongue that speaks all the languages of the earth. The members of the Council without exception said that this is the absolute right of the Imam for he is the best and holiest of men. No one could contest my right as Imam to possess the best of wives, a woman without parallel in beauty and knowledge of the world, who will accompany me in my travels and represent me at inaugural functions when required. She will put on the official attire, join in the applause and acclamations of the crowd as she stands by my side in festivals and in celebrations of victory. In defeat she will wear the white uniform of nurses, offer sweets to the wounded and the handicapped and join the widows of martyrs when they sing an anthem of praise to the dead, as they stand in the Great Hall, their eyes lifted in praise to the picture of the Imam hanging proudly from the monument to victory with his face looking humbly at the heavens. My lips mutter verses of praise to God seated on his throne in heaven, but every now and then they curl with a quick intimate smile directed at the Devil. In my ears echo the acclamations of the crowd. I raise my right hand in the air, but my lower lip hangs down over my beard with the humility proper to a holy man. There I stand tall and upright on the platform, wearing the face of the Imam. On my forehead is the mark of the faithful to God, those who believe in Him and pray for His forgiveness, and over my chest hangs the Medal of Great Victories. To my right stands my Chief of Security, and on my left is my Great Writer followed by my Leader of the Lawful Opposition. Behind are row upon row of Ministers, representatives of great powers, and personalities of state.

God is with you. Up into the air mounts the shout launched by men and women, children in the uniforms of scouts, girls dressed as nurses, soldiers in their khaki trousers, workers in

35

blue overalls, peasants, their bodies clothed in flowing robes and their heads covered in skullcaps, while popular dance troupes weave their way through the crowds, women dancing and cymbals clashing. A million voices raised in acclamation resound as one voice, which thunders out accompanied by the refrains of partriotic songs and anthems of praise, the beating of drums, rockets fired to the sun filling space with noise and vivid colours. White pigeons shoot up into the sky in flocks of fluttering wings followed by planes carrying bombs which have expired many years ago. The sound of the words, God is with you, vibrate in his ears again and again. His eyes were raised to the heavens and deep in their look was a question. If you are on my side O God, why have I suffered defeat? Why dost thou hide from me the secret of the nuclear bomb, and divulge its secrets to the enemy, to the unbelievers, why deprive thy humble servants and faithful followers from its benefits? Have mercy on me O Allah for I should not be asking thee to explain the reasons why, or the causes of thy actions. It is thy will and thy will is not to be questioned, for to question is to oppose and to oppose can only bring harm. I thought that this Satan who stands by my side would play his role of opposition within the limits prescribed by my decrees, that he would serve to bestow upon me the honourable reputation of a man of liberty and democracy. But no, he does not know his limits. He has grown arrogant and conceited, filled the newspapers with his pictures and even arranged things so that they are sometimes placed higher than mine. He smiles at me like an angel and then strikes out at me behind my back. He stands close to the representatives of the Great Powers during celebrations and keeps shooting glances at my harem.

My new wife has studied Political Science overseas. She has a theory about the art of ruling, about the art of taming men. She says to me: Hold your stick in the middle and refrain from hitting out with it all the time. Pat people over the shoulder like a mother sometimes, and at others beat down with it hard on the head. Remember you and I will distribute roles between the two of us. If you hit hard I will arrive with an angel's smile upon my face. But if you forgive

36

or compromise I will raise the stick high up, or pull on the reins until the bit cuts deep into the mouth.

I said to her: You take care of the opposition and of Hizb Al Shaitan.

I will tame the men, she said. A man is like a child even if he lifts the flag of rebellion high up to the sky. But woman is the reptile. Woman is the snake even if she wraps a veil around her face and joins the ranks of Hizb Allah.

But my enemies are all men, said I. Ever since we were children they have nurtured hatred for me deep in their hearts. Amongst the women I have only two enemies. An old woman whom I put aside with my old clothes and other things from bygone times, and an illegitimate daughter born out of a moment of rashness and numerous cups of wine.

Your old wife has broken wings, she said, and is no longer able to fly, but your daughter is the real danger, for in her heart she bears an ancient grudge and has decided that sooner or later you must die.

But a daughter would never kill her father even if he rapes her like a wolf, said I. She loves me. In her hearts of hearts she has always been loyal to me because I am her father.

You, she said, are the one who is in love, the one who stands under the lights and the lights are blinding your eyes. Look carefully. There she stands hiding at the back of the crowd waiting for a chance to strike, to aim at you and kill in the flicker of an eye.

No one will try to kill me other than a member of Hizb Al Shaitan, or a mercenary hired by some secret party, or an enemy sent from a foreign land, said I.

Your enemies are many Imam, and the higher God helps you to rise the more numerous they become, was her reply. Do not go on to the streets without your bullet-proof vest.

God is my bullet-proof vest, I told her. He is my only shield and guide. He is my one and only protector in this life.

If bullets speak, God alone will not be enough, she said, looking me straight in the eye, to which I quickly replied: God have mercy on us for what you have said, woman. You are indeed an infidel and have not removed the cross from where it lies deep in your heart. Do you not trust in Allah's ability to protect me from all danger?

Since the night we consummated our nuptial vows I drove Christ out of my heart and put my trust in you, in Allah and His Prophet, she said. I fear for you from your enemies who hide, and I know that to prevent things from happening is better than waiting until it is too late.

But I am not going to an encounter with my enemies, said I. I am going to meet my beloved people, my dear soldiers whose hearts are overflowing with love for me and with loyalty to our sacred vows. I can hear their voices join in the mighty chorus, Long live the Imam, give him long life O God that he live for ever. Do you not hear their acclamations rising to the skies, woman?

The Body Guard

The Body Guard knew nothing about affairs of state, nor of matters related to the Imamate. His functions were well defined. They consisted in putting on the rubber face which had been made to resemble the features of the Imam, in using props and other things to give him the tall and upright figure which people had seen so often standing high up on platforms surrounded by batteries of microphones, and in making sure that on all public occasions he remained close to the Imam. No one in the whole land could possibly distinguish between the two, tell which was the false Imam from the true, except the God of heaven and the Chief of Security. Nevertheless the Body Guard never allowed his senses to be lulled into a feeling that all was well. His ears kept turning themselves in all directions so that if at any moment he perceived what might resemble the sound of bullets being fired from a gun, he could immediately throw himself in front of the Imam and with his body intercept whatever bullet was destined for the One and Only Ruler. Thus he would die with that feeling of sublime happiness accorded only to he who has chosen to die a martyr for a great cause, who knows that the key of Paradise hanging around his neck will serve him well and that all he will have to do is insert it in the door and enter, upon which he will find himself in the presence of the Prophet and the other martyrs who have arrived before him. He would also die happy in the knowledge that after death his wife promoted to the status of Widow of the Great Martyr will be provided with a special double pension and decorated with an Order of the Third Degree.

On the servant list our man was officially described as the Body Guard. Only people with unique qualities could aspire to occupy this very special post, which entailed great risks and was very important since it required total devotion and loyalty to the Imam and complete faith in him. It was clear that such qualities could only be found in someone who had abandoned all use of his mind or who did not possess a capacity for reasoning at all. It had to be so since any attempt to think could lead to hesitation and hesitation even if only for a moment could mean the end of the Imam. Once a bullet was fired, if the Body Guard was slow in throwing himself forwards to intercept it with his body, the greatest of catastrophes would ensue. A complete lack of any capacity to think was therefore considered the first and foremost requisite in whoever applied for the post. The Imam himself chose his Body Guard. The applicants were made to stand in a line as he sat on his swinging canopy in the palace gardens. The choice was made after careful testing of the applicants' brain cells, and the results were registered on a sheet of the whitest paper. Any mark or black dot on the paper could immediately arouse doubt as to the applicant's suitability since it would signify that one of the cells in his brain was still functioning.

Are you prepared to die for the Imam?

Yes, with the greatest of happiness.

All of them said yes. There was not a single no. But the Imam did not trust what people said. He believed only in the elecronic apparatus which alone was capable of distinguishing between truth and lies. It was a difficult test, and only one person in a million could hope to succeed in passing it. After testing of the brain came testing of the body, and this was no less difficult. Many things had to be tested. The capacity of the ear to stretch and strain itself to the full so as to hear the sound of the bullet before it was fired from the gun. The capacity of the body to encounter death and to take on the form and consistency of the Imam's body so that the two became indistinguishable. The agility required to drop suddenly and die, without drawing anybody's attention to what was happening or giving anyone the slightest chance to realize that a bullet had been fired from a gun, especially as the sound was usually muffled by the use of one of those modern devices fitted to guns used in assassinating leaders.

40

Besides, the acclamations of the crowd were so high that they made it impossible to hear the gun being fired even if it did make a sound. God is with you, they cried.

The Imam lifted his face to the sky and fixed his attention on it, his mind straying for a moment from what was happening on earth. But in this split second of time the gun went off. The Body Guard leapt to receive the bullet in his body with open arms. He fell to the ground at the Imam's feet without drawing the attention of any one of the people standing around. His body seemed to evaporate, to melt in no time, only to be replaced by another body with exactly the same contours and lines and with exactly the same rubber face which he was wont to wear over his own face so that he remained the living image of the Imam and made it impossible for anyone to distinguish between the true and false Imam even if it were his own wife.

Every time the Body Guard walked out of the door of his house he felt it would be for the last time, that he would not return. Yet he walked out of his own free will, his heart overflowing with happiness at the thought that he was going to his death carrying the key of Paradise around his neck. It hung from a fine silver chain and was cut like a fish tail with sharp indentations. Sometimes he used to wonder how he was going to open the door to Paradise with this key. Was Paradise like a house with a door leading into it? Would Radwan, the doorkeeper of Paradise, let him open the door with his key? Many questions went through his mind as he stood there with the acclamations of the crowd echoing in his ears. The cells of his brain kept chasing them away but they would return again. No one noticed how he stood there frowning slightly as though his brain was thinking away. The electric current had been cut off for some time and the electronic detector was not in functioning order.

The Chief of Security fastened his eyes on the back rows of the crowd, but the Imam kept a careful watch on the sky. Meanwhile the head of the Body Guard maintained itself in exactly the same position as that of the Imam, gazing up into the heavens all the time. When the Imam waved his hand at the crowd, the Body Guard managed to repeat the same movement without lagging behind. No one could

41

possibly detect any difference between the two. The Imam had a characteristic way of walking over the land. He moved with a slight limp, the right foot coming down more heavily on the ground than the left one, for whereas the bones of his right leg were quite straight, the bones of his left leg were slightly bowed. But somehow the Body Guard seemed able to advance with exactly the same gait. It was said that the curvature in the left leg of the Imam had been caused by a lack of calcium in his mother's milk. The poor woman had never heard of the affliction called rickets and thought that the deformity in her son's leg was caused by the evil eye, so she tied a blue bead round his neck with a string and dressed him in the clothes of a girl.

The Imam had the ability to be in two places at the same time but no one except the Body Guard knew his secret. The Imam would whisper something in his ear. Very often it was an order to replace him in some meeting or celebration, or in one of the sessions of the Advisory Council, or during the Friday prayer at the mosque, or in an official visit to some overseas country.

Thus on many occasions he preceded important personalities of state and Ministers, walking at a short distance in front of them, yet no one had the slightest suspicion that he was not the Imam. In fact the Body Guard himself had ended up by believing that he was really the Imam. Even if at moments a fleeting doubt happened to cross his mind, it was soon dispelled by the acclamations of the crowd. He would step ahead at the exact pace required, wearing the rubber face of the Imam, his face lifted to the sky with pride, as though he was absorbed in the issues of the time. On certain days he could be seen receiving ambassadors, or experts, or visitors from foreign countries, with a serene calm. At the inauguration of a new orphanage he cut the coloured ribbon with the pair of silver scissors presented to him on the platter. At meetings of the Advisory Council he remained just as silent as the Imam, listening to the reports made by the Ministers. Every now and then he would nod his head in understanding, or his eyes would stray upwards as though he was lost in deep thought. No one noticed that he was not thinking of anything, that his mind had abandoned his body on the seat of the Imam and had fled to the ground floor. There he took off his rubber face, rubbed his nose flattened by the pressure of the other nose he always wore, and slipped out of the back door of the palace with the servants, hiding himself under his real face to avoid discovery. Once outside he jumped into a bus before it stopped, then jumped out of it before the ticket collector came up to where he stood, and walked leisurely down the narrow lanes kicking at the pebbles with his pointed shoes until he reached the house where he was going.

His mother received him with a warm embrace, winding her arms tightly around him. He could recognize the smell of freshly baked bread and dung that clung closely to her clothes. How could you forget your mother for so long, for twenty years or more? Have twenty years passed since I was here last time? Was I not here yesterday, mother? He who covers his body with the days is always naked. He who keeps his distance from the crown is always king,* she says. He sits on her knee and she rocks him up and down telling him about all the things which have happened since he was last here. This winter all my chickens died of diarrhoea, and your aunt, may God have mercy on her, was taken ill with cholera and expired after a few days. Your uncle went on a pilgrimage to Mecca and never returned. Your female cousin was bitten by a mad dog and immediately after that your father visited me in a dream and said that he was waiting for me up there in Paradise. My son, have you forgotten what you promised me? Where is my ticket to Mecca?

He buried his head in her bosom. No mother, it's not that I have forgotten, but you know how it is with all these problems of being Imam and which seem to be without solution. Allah alone is all powerful and no one but He can do anything. You know, mother, this question of foreign debts and all. Then the struggle between the Great Powers which nobody can stop, and the preparations for a space war. Besides, I've had trouble with Hizb Al Shaitan, in fact with almost all its members. They are sons and daughters of

* A popular saying, the first part of which means that time (days) fly by before you can even feel them, that time is an illusion.

43

fornication, may God punish them with Hell fire. And this pain I feel here in my chest just under your hand. Her fingers are hard and cracked with toil but they touch him gently over his wound. It is a deep wound which goes right through from the back to his heart. She fills it up with ashes from the mud oven and with coarse grains of coffee, to help it heal quickly, and he goes to sleep in her arms, her voice sounding like a distant sob as she sings her sad song.

Her deep strong voice reached him from afar as he stood on the platform wearing the face of the Imam just a moment before his fall. Its tones were wafted to his ears like a voice in a far-away dream, or like a dream within a dream. Many were the times when in his sleep he had dreamt that he was dreaming. He would awaken in the middle of his dream, then fall asleep again only to dream once more that he was dreaming. In this dream he put on his rubber face and descended the stairs of the palace like someone walking in his sleep. Outside a car was waiting for him. He got into it and it drove him through the streets while he waved to his people. In the meetings of the Advisory Council the Ministers would see him as he sat there listening attentively without hearing, shaking his head in understanding without understanding. He scratched his head from time to time as though thinking deeply, lost to what was going on around. But he was not thinking, for thinking was not required of those who occupied the post he occupied.

The sound of guns being fired echoed in the air with a deafening noise. Suddenly everything was enveloped in darkness. The blood froze in his veins, for ever since he was a child he had feared the darkness, the acclamations of the crowd and the sound of drums beating the salute to victory. At such moments no one sees the bullet when it is fired from the gun, and no one but he falls to the ground. He alone is the one who dies. His body drops down between his feet and after a short while it is gone. Nobody sees it go, it just goes, and power is shifted from one to the other as fast as the rubber face is shifted from one face to the other. As for the people, they do not feel that anything has happened, that a change has occurred, for the Imam remains where he is, standing high up on the elevated platform, his head raised to the heavens. The rockets celebrating the Big Feast continue to be fired, and the acclamations continue to resound, filling the air with one great shout. God is with you.

The Two Faces

At a distance my childhood looks as though it was a happy childhood. Time consumes pain and there remains only the joy. Tears of sadness wash the eyes and make them see better than before. I still see my sister's face, and her eyes shine into my eyes in the dark of night. She takes me in her arms and her bosom is soft and smooth like a mother. As for my brother, I carry him around with me wherever I go like the odour of my body. I can smell him in my sweat, in the perfume of my flowers. His body is my body, his flesh is my flesh, his sweat is my sweat. He and I are one, inseparable.

In the nursing school I see myself wearing a white dress, my hair rolled up inside a white cap. I move from one bed to the other like an angel, light as a feather, my feet hardly touching the ground. I am a spirit without body, without substance, a tall and slender shadow passing by. My voice is a whisper, my breathing deep like a child. My breasts under the bodice of my white tunic are small and defiant and round. I have a small white bed in a big dormitory and by my side is a wooden drawer with my name, Bint Allah, painted on it. Next to me is my sister Nemat Allah. Her face is thin, her features wan, but when she sees me a light shines in her eyes.

The school for nurses was a huge old building with walls which had blackened over time. It was the only school of its kind, for only orphans without father or mother were allowed to apply. Adjoining the nursing school was the military hospital. It had shining varnished windows and big terraces closed in with glass which overlooked the river. Across the river was another huge construction with a history as old as the history of slavery in our land. Its walls too had blackened with time, and year after year so many layers of dust had covered them that they had become the same colour as the earth and looked as though they had risen from its bowels. The windows were high and covered with long bars of iron like a prison. The eyes of children could be seen as they looked out, shining like stars in a world of night. They were known as the children of God, but the term used in official documents to describe them was illegitimate children. Behind the children's home was an open space where the ground was flat and pale yellow but at its furthest confines the ground sloped upwards into a low flat hill covered by cactuses and thorn trees which people were in the habit of calling wild plants because they thought that such plants could only have grown against the will of God. In the shelter of the hill was still another enormous building, its age as old as that of Satan on earth. Its black walls rose so high up in the sky that they pierced through the clouds, defying heaven. Its windows were tall, and covered with long iron bars exactly like the windows of the children's home. From behind these iron bars one could see the faces of women looking out, their hair gathered in the folds of a handkerchief knotted around their heads, or left to float loosely in the air. It was always long and tangled, matted from lying in bed, and through it crept swarms of lice moving on thread-like legs, yet it shone under the sun with the bright colours of the rainbow. This place was commonly known as the House of Joy, but in the files of the Chief of Security it was referred to as the Prostitutes' House.

From her window in the School of Nurses Bint Allah could not see the river or the low flat hill behind it. The huge military hospital filled the universe, blocking everything out completely except a small patch of sky which looked down at her from over the top of its walls, and a slender ray of light from the sun which reached her before it set at the end of each day.

I was not allowed to look out of the windows for the terraces of the military hospital faced the windows of the dormitories where we slept. The army doctors leaned over the balustrades to take a look at the girls below. They smiled or nodded their heads or whistled. On their chests they displayed rows of coloured ribbons, and on their shoulders were shining pieces of metal shaped like stars. Their heads

47

were always covered by a military cap. At night after the final bell had rung my sister would lean her head over the edge of the bed and tell me a story about love. From under her bodice out came the photograph of a man in military uniform. We examined it together in the dim light. He wore his military cap squarely on the head, and on his chest shone a rounded metal disc. The jutting peak of his cap cast a grey shadow over the upper part of his face. It hid the look in his eyes and the shape of his nose. Under his nose was a square moustache carefully trimmed, which reminded me of Hitler. She would kiss the picture, push it quickly back into her bodice close to her heart, and then start to tell me her story all over again.

He had been hit by a bullet in his chest and she stood beside him as he lay in his bed. He called her my tender angel and her fingers were gentle over his wound. She spent the nights at his side and whenever he opened his eyes she was there standing or sitting close to his bed. If she left him to get some sleep a single ring of the bell would bring her back to his side. If the bell did not ring she crept back into his room on tiptoe and waited for his eyes to open. Whenever the blankets slipped slightly to one side she set them right. If he was thirsty she gave him something to drink and if he wished she read to him before he slept, verses from the Holy Book of God, or items from the newspapers about the war, for those were the only things which interested him. When he spoke to her it was always about the war. He had killed three men, but the fourth had managed to lodge a bullet in his chest and get away under cover of night. On Victory Day the Imam decorated him with a medal for his courage in battle. But for him all this was just a normal thing, for he had been trained to kill even as a child. He had a gun with which he killed the birds in spring as they stood on the branches looking down at him. He steadied the gun against his shoulder, took careful aim at the middle of the head before he pulled the trigger and the bird would drop with a single shot and die on the ground without a quiver.

I put my arms around her and held her tight. Her body was small and slender like a bird and in my heart was a great yearning for a mother. I buried my head between her breasts and wept. Then drying my eyes I said: I do not want him to kill you with one of his ugly bullets. In her eyes was a strange glitter when she said: I know he will kill me but it will be with love not with a bullet.

I knew nothing about love. My heart was full of a deep yearning for two arms that would hold me in a tight embrace without causing me any pain. Every time I caught the look on Nemat Allah's face my eyes shone with a tender light. In the drawer next to my bed were a pile of letters which I had written to someone imaginary, but deep in my heart was a fear of love and a greater fear of God. In the children's home I prayed regularly and God appeared to me in my dreams as a man. He caressed my bosom with a gentle hand and my belly became swollen with the Jesus Christ that was yet to be born. And now in the morning when I prayed, God's voice resounded in my ears full of anger. He cursed me in a loud voice and threatened to inflict cruel punishment on me. I fell on my knees and bowed my head low to the ground, entreating Him to have mercy on me. I prayed five times a day and each time I prostrated myself before Him. He would not cease to vent His wrath on me for a single moment, and at night I curled myself under the bed covers and watched Him as He approached. Now His words were no longer angry but gentle and soft-spoken and His face was as gentle as the moon on a summer's night. He rocked me in His arms, filling my heart with a love that was pure. My belly rose with a sacred pregnancy and I watched it grow slowly like a ball filling up gradually with air. I called out to Him when He turned His back on me and He swung round and started to come closer to me once more. But this time His face was completely different, a new face, sombre almost black with wrath, with eyes burning like glowing embers. I opened my mouth to scream. My body seemed pegged to the ground and I could not move. Suddenly I awakened, my body bathed in sweat, and with my pen wrote the first halting words of a letter addressed to no one. I saw God in my sleep and He had two faces. One smooth and gentle as a mother's face, and the other like the face of Satan.

The First Letters in the Alphabet of Love

We were not permitted to look out of the windows. The balconies of the military hospital overlooked the windows of the nursing school and so the military men could look down on the girls from above. The hospital buildings were huge and obstructed the light of the sun, but at the end of the day when I stood near the window a long slender ray of sunlight would reach me over one of the corners. I could feel the harsh grip of fingers over my back pulling me away from it. They were the fingers of the Head Nurse. She was a short middle-aged woman wearing a white veil and a long uniform reaching down to the ground, like a sister in a monastery. She had a rounded white face and plump hands. Over her bodice she wore three stars which hung from a chain around her neck, as well as the Order of Charity, a golden disc in the form of a brooch pinned over her left breast. Under the fine silk of her uniform, her big breasts jogged up and down. As she advanced with short quick steps over the floor they preceded her, her buttocks like two mounds of flesh bringing up the rear. The right buttock rose up when the left came down and the left buttock rose up when the right came down, as though each hemisphere was not in its place. When she was standing she kept her arms close to her body, but when she walked one arm would swing out while the other remained stuck to her side. During the day her pointed metal-tipped heels struck the tiled floor with a chinking resonance but at night she tiptoed on soundless bare feet. She made the rounds of the dormitory like a lost soul floating in the night without a body, and when she passed through the doors the flutter of her tunic was like a whisper of air. Her face was all fat without muscle but it remained completely rigid and never exhibited even the finest of tremors, like a plate of milk

50

boiled with starch. But her eyes were two balls of grey lead that moved restlessly everywhere. Overhanging each of them was a semicircular brow drawn with a fine pencil. Looked at from the side her nose pointed scornfully upwards into the air. She appeared or disappeared in the dormitories and corridors like a spirit from another world or a being never known to exist before.

When I slept at night I kept my ears strained to catch the slightest whisper in the air. I could detect the soft trailing of her tunic or the invisible pressure of her bare foot on the floor. The knob of the door would move round of its own accord as though turned by the hand of a spirit or a devil. I could see her as she slipped into the dormitory like a white shadow, moving from bed to bed inspecting the dreams of the girls while they slept, her eyes shifting from bed to bed like a pair of flashlights to make sure there was only one head in each bed. She counted the heads on her fingers like a herdsman counting his sheep. If a head was missing from a bed or if there were two heads on one bed, the alarm would be given as though we were at war.

I was in my bed, and close to me Nemat Allah lay in hers. Her eyes were wide open with a far-away staring look which never left her. Her face kept getting thinner and paler and her eyes bigger and blacker all the time. If I whispered in her ear at night she did not answer. If my lips touched her face not a muscle of her features moved. I put my arms around her frail body and fell asleep. But in the middle of the night I suddenly opened my eyes and looked at her bed. It was empty and the place at my side where she sometimes slept was empty too. I knew my way. The long passage was dark, and I walked on the edge of the wall without faltering. When I reached the end I found a closed door and behind it I heard someone moaning. I pushed the door open with my fist and for a moment could see nothing but the tiles of the floor shining dimly. But as my eyes grew used to the dark I saw her lying there in the corner of the room. She was curled up like a baby in its womb and from under her body trickled a fine thread of blood. It was dark red in colour but her fingers were as white as the moon, as though there was no more blood in them. Between her fingers I could see something

51

written in black letters on a sheet of crumpled paper held between fingers turned to stone. No one could open her fingers. What was written on the paper? asked the Head Nurse, standing in front of a line of men dressed in official uniforms with hats on their heads. I do not know, said I. The line of men looked at me and said: How can that be when she was with you day and night? She was with me day and night but she lived in another world, said I. Which world is that? they queried. I do not know for I have not been there yet, said I.

Night falls, faces melt into the dark, and the air ceases to whisper in my ears. I see her standing in the night. I open her stone-like fingers clasped around the crumpled piece of paper, hold it under the white moon and read the letter written on a surface white and pure.

The Legal Wife Will Not Go to Paradise

The acclamations of the crowd resound in my ears. Above my head is the throne of the heavens, and at my feet where I stand lies the throne of earth. I am surrounded on all sides by my men. They keep a close guard and protect me from my enemies, who are numerous and are waiting for their chance to replace me on the throne. My friends are few. They think their turn will come when I die. On my right stands my Chief of Security, who is more interested in my downfall than anyone else. On my left stands my Great Writer with his right eye fastened on the leader of Hizb Al Shaitan and his left eye fastened on my Legal Wife where she stands on the balcony reserved for the harem, surrounded by model wives and mothers of martyrs. The acclamations of the people echo in her ears, mingled with the noise of rockets shooting to the sky in celebration of the Big Feast and the sharp noise of bullets fired from a gun. She watches my face as it falls off my body but she remains standing in the same place with her right eye fastened on the throne and her left eye gazing at my life-long friend.

Ever since I was a child I have envied and hated him. He always managed to get higher grades than I did in the examinations. Besides, despite all the girls who admired him he found nobody else to go after than the girl of my dreams. He used to send her love letters and poems dedicated to her, whereas I could hardly write my name. I bestowed the title of Great Writer on him, allowed him a full page in the daily morning paper in which to publish his articles together with a picture in which he smiles out at the girls, yet despite all that he does not stay within his limits. Ever since he was a child the desires of his heart have never cooled down. There he stands by my side following the noise of all these explosions, watching my head as it falls from on high to the ground, seeing chaos let loose as though it is the end of the world, and yet he remains unmoved like a sphinx carved out of stone. Suddenly the faces of the friends and enemies I know disappear as though swallowed up by a void and are replaced by the faces of men I have never seen before. They move up closer and surround me where I lie hiding my face in the ground. One of them turns my head around and looks into my face. I hear him say: This is not the face we know. And I hear the others ask: Whose face is it then? To which he replies: God only knows.

It must be that my face looked more awesome and dignified than that of the Imam, the face of a man much greater than that of an ordinary man. For its skin was stone-white, almost bloodless, and the bones were hard as rock, rigid, unmoving. A shiver went through the men who were gathered around me and they kneeled on the ground as though in adoration. One of them came closer to me. Noticing that my face was getting darker and darker and that it was gradually changing to the colour of the earth on which I lay, he turned on his heels and ran away as fast as he could, crying out, It's the Devil, and the others followed close behind him. All of them shouted in one voice, It's the Devil, and as they ran one of them stepped on my hand, and another stepped on my medal where it lay on the ground close to my right foot. I buried my face in the ground so that no one should see me and suddenly I felt a gentle hand touch my head. When I peered out cautiously from between my lids I began to see faces which I had seen somewhere before. But when they lifted my head up from the ground and looked at my face none of them seemed to recognize me. At that moment I heard a voice whose smooth tones sounded familiar to me. It resembled the voice of my Legal Wife or of the Chief of Security and said: No it's not him. Then another voice which could have been that of my Great Writer or of the Leader of the Official Opposition cried out suddenly: God has saved him, God is on his side. And immediately on every side voices started to acclaim me. Long live the Imam. The guns of victory fired a salvo and the drums beat out a loud refrain.

I saw my Legal Wife descend from the balcony walking with a slow serene step and the great calm of a lion. But as soon as she disappeared out of my sight she started to run on her pointed high heels towards the bedroom. The curtains had been drawn over the windows and my body lay on the bed surrounded by my legitimate and illegitimate sons and daughters. The Minister of Health was sprinkling disinfectant over my body to prevent it from rotting. In the adjoining room the men I depended on in Hizb Allah were busy dividing up whatever I had left behind me between themselves. When my Legal Wife entered the room her eyes immediately fell on the face of my illegitimate daughter who was standing beside me. On her right stood her mother Gawaher and on her left stood my first wife. The atmosphere before she arrived had been calm and pleasant. I lay in bed holding on to my illegitimate daughter's smooth hand, kissing it every now and then. But my Legal Wife leapt on us like a tiger and suddenly all the faces that were gathered around me disappeared, and I was left alone with the face of my Legal Wife standing beside me. She removed all the marriage and kingly rings from my fingers, emptied my pockets of small change, divested me of my official dress and buried me in a pit dug in the palace gardens.

But the people continued to clamour out my name unceasingly as I lay in the burial pit, and as I stood high up on the elevated platform delivering my speech on the occasion of the Big Feast. No one except my Legal Wife and my Chief of Security realized that I was in two places at the same time. The rockets continued to shoot up into the sky in celebration of the Big Feast, and the acclamations of the crowds continued to resound.

It occurred to no one that I was not the Imam. I myself could not believe that I was the Imam and the Leader of these people. I closed my eyes and abandoned myself to the enjoyable feeling of being the Leader without being the Leader. Thus I could move about freely without needing to wear a bullet-proof vest and without being haunted by the fear of assassination; for I knew that I had already been assassinated before, and it was better for me to be a dead Imam rather than not to be the Imam at all. Now my new name would be the Imam Martyr, and this new name would bestow a new greatness on me. I had become above death and could sit on my throne without fearing my enemies or my friends. As a martyr I had developed the ability to rise up in the air, to fly from the first world to the second or even the third world. I no longer feared either the Great or Small Powers, and I could sit opposite the greatest of leaders with my right leg crossed over my left leg.* In the morning I drank my coffee in the Lands of the North and at midday I had lunch in the Lands of the South. Then in the evening after the day was over I could spend a quiet night under the ground in the House of Joy with Gawaher. Sitting by my side was my life-long friend and we drank toast after toast to love and friendship. I had bestowed a title on him and he had a full page in which to write, with his picture at the top framed in a box. Every Thursday we stayed up all night talking about the memories of our youth.

Do you remember the girl we fucked together?

I slapped his thigh with the palm of my hand and roared with laughter. He slapped me on my thigh in turn and his laughter rang out as heartily as mine. But a moment later he eyed me hesitantly and his laughter subsided as though he suddenly realized that he had ventured to slap the thigh of the Imam. His hand remained suspended in the air but I slapped his thigh a second time and burst out laughing just as loudly, remembering all the while how he used to sit beside me in school dressed in his expensive woollen trousers and hit me on the buttocks from behind, right where I held my hand over the hole in my trousers trying to hide it. So I laughed in great hilarity for the third time and slapped him on his thigh again where it lay inside the leg of his trousers, thin and tense like the thigh of a tiger. Then I said: Do you remember the name of that girl? He laughed noisily and in the midst of his laughter I heard him say: Of course, her name was Gawaher. Her body was as white as milk and her skin was so fine that the flesh underneath it showed through. Her eyes were big and black like the eyes of the maidens

* In the tradition, to cross one's legs in front of another person is a sign of equality and is considered by elders as disrespect.

56

waiting for us in Paradise. At these words my mind took a sudden leap out of this world into the hereafter. I saw Paradise like a vast expanse of green. I lay on the sweet soft grass near the river and all around me naked maidens floated in its waters, their bodies shining in the sun. My eyes travelled slowly between their beautiful faces until I was sure that my Legal Wife was not among them. My voice rang out again and again in peals of laughter and this time I slapped him on the thigh with a resounding whack. How many maidens is each believer allowed? I asked. Either seventy or seventy-seven, I don't remember exactly, he said. God alone knows the exact number. But how many maidens are allowed if it's the Leader of the Faithful, the One and Only Imam? I asked.

The Great Writer laughed even more loudly than before and let his imagination run wild, volunteering a figure which was a pure guess. But the Imam possessed an imagination even more fertile than that of the Great Writer, and his mind got carried away. What about our legal wives? His life-long friend pondered over the matter for a long moment before he said: Our legal wives will never go to Paradise. But what if one of them happens to slip in somehow, asked the Imam insistently, then what? God will replace her with a young maiden, affirmed the Great Writer. In Paradise there is no place for legal wives. For if it were not so, what difference would there be between our life on earth and life in Paradise?

Statutory Treachery

When I learnt that my sister had died in the war I recalled that I had not seen my mother's face since the night I was born. In the orphanage we had an old grandmother whom we called Siti Al Haja.* We gathered around her in the evenings and listened to her tales about djinns and about sirens who had the bodies of women and the tails of fish and swam along the shores of the sea at night. When a siren set her hands on a man she used sorcery to change him into another creature, into a catfish or a young calf or a sheep or any other animal of a lower order. If he had been changed into a sheep he would go round bleating in a low voice, looking for another woman against whose leg he would rub himself. This woman had to possess the secrets of sorcery so that she could unravel the incantations of the woman at whose hands he had been changed into a sheep. Thus she could return him to his original state as a man. But once he had become a man again he would strut over the land full of his manliness, forgetting the woman who had created him, driven by his conceit to seek for another woman who in her turn would reduce him from the state of a human being to that of a monkey or a cat with no tail.

He would begin to go round again seeking after a woman sorceress, rubbing himself up against her legs, and so round and round and on and on and night after night would go the tales told by our grandmother to the children gathered around her in the dormitory. Like in *The Thousand and One Nights*, the beginning of each new tale merged with the end

* Literally, My mistress who has done the pilgrimage to Mecca. Used as a term of respect when speaking of or addressing the grandmother or an old woman with whom there is some intimacy.

of the one which had preceded it, like the night merges with the day. Her voice never ceased to echo in our ears, her story never ended before it had begun to merge into a new one. Like Scheherezad she seemed to fear even a moment's silence lest when she paused at some point in her tale her heart would stop beating, for Scheherezad knew her life would cease the moment she ceased speaking. Who was Scheherezad, Siti Al Haja? we asked, and immediately she picked up her story again. The husband left his wife to go to another woman and when he returned at the end of the day he found her in the arms of his black slave. He killed his wife and swore an oath that from then on in order to avenge himself for her treachery, every night he would kill a virgin in his bed. The husband was a white-skinned man of noble descent and he had occupied the thone of the earth since an early age. Every night he buckled his sword around his waist and implored God in heaven to have mercy on him, for how could a woman prefer a black slave to the King Shahrayar himself. He could hear a voice speaking as though it arose from deep down inside him, a voice which resembled that of his father and which said: Because women are born treacherous like their mother Eve.

At this point I interrupted her as she went on telling her tale and said: But the King was betraying his wife with a black woman slave. She looked at me askance and said: What matter girl, the treachery of men is allowable by divine law, as God Himself has said. But the treachery of women is inspired by Satan.

When I was a child I wondered why it was that the skin of kings was always white whereas that of slaves was always black. I myself had a dark skin and I wondered whether I was descended from a breed of slaves. When I asked Siti Al Haja she spat into the neck of her black robe to chase away the Devil and said: O God verily I seek protection in thee from Satan the accursed enemy. May evil always be far away from us and let no doubts assail us. You my child are descended from the breed of masters not of slaves.

Ever since I first opened my eyes on life in the orphanage they have called me Bint Allah. And after Siti Al Haja died I never stopped staring at my dark skin in the mirror and wondering about it. In my dreams my father always appeared to me with a skin as white as that of King Shahrayar. From where then did I get this dark skin? Did my mother betray my father with a black slave? Or am I the daughter of Satan and not the daughter of God as my name says?

I can see myself trying to escape in the night, running as fast as I can with my dog Marzouk close behind me. Men wearing military caps are close on my heels and bringing up the rear are a pack of dogs, their panting breath rising like a mist. I quickly climb the hill up between the river and the sea. I had almost given them the slip, was almost out of their reach, when I halted for a moment, seized by a yearning to fill my lungs with the air of open spaces. Since I was a child this yearning for the pure air of this place had never left me. In it was the warm odour of my mother's flesh before she died. Here was the footprint left by my father on the earth before he fled leaving her behind. Yes I could have escaped from those who were hunting me down had I not remembered all these things as I trod over the ground. And just at the moment when I halted to inhale the odours of my life the bullet struck me in the back. They always hit me in the back, never stand up to face me from the front. But before the letters of the alphabet had faded from my mind, before my memory had gone completely dead, I had the time to hear them say: All this is the fruit of sin. He who kills her will be rewarded handsomely, both in this world and later on in Paradise.

Everything Happened Suddenly

My head was high up in the sky. I was wearing the face of
the Imam. Over my chest hung a row of medals and through
my fingers moved the sacred rosary of prayer beads which
had been sent to me directly from the Kaaba*. The lights of
the first and second worlds flashed like rounded mirrors,
surrounding me from all directions. And the acclamations of
the peoples in the third and fourth worlds echoed in my ears
with a roaring sound. Long live the Imam, Defender of the
Shariat. My face in the mirrors around me was multiplied
into a hundred faces less one, into ninety-nine faces, like the
ninety-nine sacred names of God. Every time I moved my
head to one side or the other I could see my face become
many faces all at once. There I was high up under the lights,
seated on the throne in the midst of my supporters in Hizb
Allah and in the official opposition Hizb Al Shaitan, and
around us were the representatives of the Greater and Lesser
Powers and the flying banners of liberty and democracy
fluttering in the wind. My voice rolled out on a thousand
microphones as I delivered my speech celebrating our great
victory, while in the air burst the coloured rockets of the Big
Feast. I was drunk with exhilaration not with wine, swaying
from side to side so that at a certain moment my face
suddenly slipped off and dropped to the ground between my
feet, almost rolling under my throne, and just as suddenly
legs began to run hither and thither and feet stepped on my
foot, and suddenly my seat lay on the ground with its four
legs pointing to the sky, and I peered to one side then the
other wondering what had happened so suddenly.

The Leader of the Official Opposition was standing close

* The black stone around which pilgrims to Mecca circle seven times.

to the Imam, separated from him only by the Chief of Security, when suddenly he heard a voice asking whether the Day of Judgement had just come. He realized that it was the voice of the Imam and that the Imam was now lying under the seat of his throne a short distance from where he stood. The Leader of the Official Opposition suddenly started to exhibit more intelligence than he usually did, and made the correlation between the available seats in Noah's Ark, the discovery of nuclear energy and the Day of Judgement. The Great Writer suddenly put his head between his feet and closed his eyes in eternal rest, but awakening for a moment he peered cautiously between his lids and said that to think about the Day of Judgement with a worldly mind was not permissible according to the Shariat, that it was not possible to reach any conclusions about it except through the word of God as written in the Koran, adding that he who reads the Koran carefully will discover that the Day of Judgement is an event which does not only concern the terrestrial globe and the peoples living on it but the whole universe, for God Almighty hath said: And His trumpets will be blown unto the wall, and all who are in the heavens and on the earth shall be struck down with lightning, verily, except those He wishes to save. These are the words of God and they brook neither opposition nor even discussion, be it from the Official Opposition or from the Illegal Opposition and clandestine movements. For the Day of Judgement will encompass the whole universe including the heavens and the earth and by the will of God the only exception shall be his heir and representative on earth, the one and only Imam. This in so far as our worldly life is concerned. The words of Allah however also show that the inhabitants of the planets and stars, of the sun and the moon and of other heavenly bodies, will share the same fate as the dwellers on earth since they shall all face a sudden death. The words of God make it clear that the Day of Judgement will descend upon all of us suddenly, for God Almighty Himself has said: And did they believe that Allah will send them a cloud to blind them and make it such that they shall taste suffering at his hands, and that the Day of Judgement shall descend upon them suddenly? God has no need of things like nuclear radiations to bring the Hour of Judgement when the time has come nor does He lack the wherewithal to destroy the whole universe suddenly.

The eyes of the Imam shone with admiration for the eloquence exhibited by his Great Writer, the extraordinary scope of his religious culture and his extensive knowledge of Shariat. The eyes of the Leader of the Official Opposition were quick to reflect the same admiration but it was soon replaced by a dark look of jealousy almost akin to hatred. He launched himself on a long speech, longer than the speech which had been made by the Great Writer, in an attempt to prove that the relationship between the Day of Judgement and nuclear radiation was not excluded even if this was not mentioned anywhere in the text of the Koran. The Chief of Security picked himself up from the ground and started to brush off the particles of dust from his coat. They floated off into the air, shining brightly as though charged with some kind of radiation. At this sight he suddenly started to run as fast as he could, leaving the leaders of Hizb Allah and Hizb Al Shaitan lying on the ground. They lay there inert, without movement, as though abandoning their fate to the will of God. Meanwhile the Great Writer was following what the Leader of the Opposition was saying, his mouth open with admiration at the courage of this man who had dared to speak of the existence of a possible relationship between nuclear radiation and the advent of the Day of Judgement without there being any mention of it in the Koran. A moment later the Great Writer and the Leader of the Official Opposition could be seen as they exchanged a smile extending from ear to ear on their faces lying between their feet on the ground.

The Imam however continued to be silent, not pronouncing even a single word. Noticing his silence they closed their mouths tightly and refrained from saying anything further, for the word of the Imam was always final and brooked no doubt or opposition of any kind. Seeing that the Imam continued to say nothing as though he had decided to maintain eternal silence, the Leader of the Opposition was encouraged to pose a question. Almost to his own surprise he heard himself ask whether the Imam existed or not. For a moment it crossed his mind that such a question could be considered a heresy and was akin to asking whether God existed or not. But he quickly realized that there was absolutely no heresy in what he had said, for on the contrary it was a proof of his deep-rooted devotion and endless loyalty to the Imam since he was only trying to buttress the faith which comes from the heart with the reason of the mind. In fact the day came when his question was cited as an historic event, despite the fact that it is something which every child in the world has asked at one time or another without being made to appear as one of the heroes in the movements of popular opposition. Nevertheless the Great Writer sent him an envious look from where his face lay on the ground under his seat, and then took himself off to his fourth wife smiling from ear to ear.

That night, comfortably in bed, he swore a triple oath of divorce if it was proved that anyone else but he had dared to peer through his lids in order to witness with his own eyes the happenings of that historic moment. For indeed not a single member of Hizb Allah or Hizb Al Shaitan had had the courage to do what he did. All of them had remained with their eyelids tightly closed all the time, as though they had died suddenly, all of them except the Chief of Security who had disappeared suddenly, leaving no trace behind him.

Ecstasy of Love

I lost my sister Nemat Allah while still in the nursing school. She sacrificed her life for love. My brother Fadl Allah went to war and lost his life in defence of his country. I do not want to be a victim, nor do I want to go through life blindfolded. I wake up in the middle of the night and learn what I have to learn by heart so that I can repeat it the next day in the examination. Came graduation day and with it the distribution of Certificates of Obedience and Service. Those that pass well in the examination are awarded the title of the Perfect Servant. They are dressed up in special white uniforms and a bandage is tied round their hair. They walk behind one another in a line and when they come near the platform bow respectfully. Seated on the platform are the important women of state, the wife of the Imam seated on a high-backed chair in their midst. On her right is the president of all charitable societies wearing her rubber face and on her left side is the Head Nurse wearing the Medal of Duty and Charity pinned on her breast. Behind come rows of other lesser women, the widows of martyrs, ideal mothers, volunteer charity workers. They all look the same and it is impossible to distinguish between them. They sit without movement, their faces serious, unsmiling, their hands clasped together over their bosoms as though hiding something. If the wife of the Imam stands up they immediately rise to their feet in a single movement, their hands still held over their bosoms. I approach the platform with a slow funereal step. The new wife of the Imam looks shorter to me when she is standing up than when she is sitting down. Her head wrapped in an imported silk veil barely appears above the rostrum. Attached round her veil is a diamond tiara which scintillates in the light. When my eyes move downwards

65

from her head I can see a necklace and further down a brooch pinned over her left breast. On her arms are rows of bracelets and on her fingers she wears many rings so that every time she moves the universe seems to tremble with the light of a thousand flashing stars.

I had witnessed a similar scene before when I finished my schooling in the children's home. In the place occupied now by the wife of the Imam was a man. I can barely remember him. He had a big head which was completely bald but his chest was covered in hair. At that time the new wife was taller, and her hair, cut very short, remained completely exposed for everyone to see. The women of the charitable associations all looked like one another. They had square fleshy bodies and small heads around which their hair was wound closely and attached by rows of hairpins. Their feet were small and plump and their legs short so that seated on their chairs their feet did not reach the ground but remained dangling in the air, swinging slightly to and fro. When they walked their pointed high heels resounded with a metallic noise on the floor.

When my turn came to be awarded the certificate I walked up to the platform. A smooth hand moved out towards me glittering with a galaxy of stars. The square bodies of the other women stood up on either side, balancing themselves on the high pointed heels, their plump white hands clasped together over their bosoms. With every certificate or prize awarded their hands would detach themselves slowly from their bosoms to meet another hand midway in the air and the sound of applause would roll out like the halting hoarse breath of some mammoth creature choking to death. As I took the certificate in my hands I felt an electric current pass from the tips of her fingers up my arm and into my body. My heart leapt against my ribs and I threw myself forwards with great enthusiasm, waving the flag in the air high over my head, shouting at the top of my voice, Allah is great. Long live my country and its Leader the Imam. My sister sacrificed her life for one man, but I shall live for the people of my land. Either complete independence for our country or death in the struggle for our land.

During the day I moved from one wounded man to the

66

other, carrying a pot for urine and another for stools. At night I kept wide-awake straining my ears to catch a moan. I could see his face as he turned it towards me in the dim light. It was thin and pale and wan. Over his chest there was a deep wound and from his eyes looked out a tender yearning. In the dark of night I go towards him and say: Fadl Allah was at the war front, did you see him there? Is he still alive? Who is Fadl Allah? he asked. Is he your husband? He is my milk brother* and he was with me in the orphanage, I said. Then I fell silent. Why are you silent? he said. What shall I say? Tell me about yourself, he said. But what can I tell you? Tell me everything, he said.

But I did not know what to say. My life seemed full of secrets and yet when I started to talk it looked empty as though there was nothing in it to talk about. He surrounded me with his arms like a mother and whispered to me, Go to sleep, and as I slept all my fears slipped away from me. I began to talk about myself and each time I recounted something my tongue became freer and freer and my heart grew lighter and lighter. My body seemed to be flying like a body without weight. As I climbed higher and higher up the hill a gasp escaped my lips. I had always dreamt of going up to the top of the hill. For twenty long years, ever since I had been born, I had continued to see the hill between the river and the sea, there where my mother stood waiting for me. I could never forget the smell of the air, nor of the damp earth under my palms, nor could I forget the tree and the rock and the slope of the hill rising up. Here was my land, my country. Its smells were the smell of my life, strong and penetrating. I opened my arms, filled my lungs with a deep breath of air like the first breath of life at the moment of birth, like the last breath of life at the moment of death. And for the first time since I was born I took in everything in one deep breath, the smell of the sea, of salt water, of iodine, of seaweed and molluscs and fresh fish. I abandoned myself to the sea air, let it seep into me, fill me up, drown me in its softness. Its white waves rose up in the night reaching to the sky, enfolding me

* Children breast-fed by the same woman; foster-brother.

like the arms of God. And he was by my side holding me in his arms and saying:

Do you like fish grilled on charcoal?

I love it.

Do you prefer the head of the fish or its tail?

I like both of them.

His laughter rang out, filling the universe like the laughter of children, like an oyster shell opening its lips to desire. The air of the sea filled her with a lust for life, with a deep hunger hungry for everything. All her senses were suddenly awakened like waves in wonderful turmoil. The stars glittering over the sea were like lighted pearls. The rustle of leaves, the sound of the waves, the whisper of the wind, joined in a single call going deep. Her black eyes opened wide in abandonment to the ecstasy of love, to the moment when everything else is excluded. Then when it is over she closes her eyes and sleeps on his chest like a child being rocked slowly, and his voice wafted to her from a distance whispers, I love you.

When Love Was Blind

I lived in the ecstasy of love with closed eyes, unable to see him. I felt my heart grow within me big like the disc of the sun. My body was a mollusc opening its lips with desire, the sea air playing with my senses, his voice echoing like a soft whisper in my ears. It came to me from a distance like the gentle voice of a mother calling to me. The stars were like diamonds in the night. But I still walked in line with the other nurses, bearing my title of Perfect Servant. When victory was celebrated I still shouted in unison with them: Glory to God, to our country and to our one and only Imam. Carried away by love and a burning enthusiasm I forgot that my sister had been sacrificed on the altar of love and that my brother had gone to the front never to return. I said to myself, love is life not death and to defend my country is a part of love.

At the war front I advanced in the front lines carrying my gun on my shoulder, aiming carefully at the enemy, ready to die at any moment. But at night I and my companions ran as fast as we could, and once we started to run we never stopped. I ran on and on and then jumped into a trench to hide. Then I started to run again until I reached a trench once more. Then rising out of the depths of the earth I continued to run on and on. In the dark I glimpsed the face of the enemy and this time I knew for certain it was the face of the enemy. There could be no mistake at all. I held my gun against my shoulder, took careful aim at a spot midway between his eyes and pulled the trigger. His face fell off his body and landed on the ground, and after that I could hear them chasing me for their shoes made a clinking sound. I thought they were the enemy so I continued to run. But there, where the hill slopes down between the river and the sea, I came to a halt. Here was a place where I felt I could be safe. I knew the ground, knew the odour of the trees, and the water flowing down. I walked slowly and as I took deep breaths of the air I could hear their footsteps treading on the ground. I said to myself, they are my friends, they are the soldiers of my country led by the Chief of Security and he brings with him the decoration of merit bestowed upon me for bravery by the Imam. When they struck me in the back with something, I turned around to face them overcome with surprise.

Why do you aim your bullets at me? Did I not kill our country's enemy?

They said: You killed our country's friend.

But until yesterday he was an enemy, I said.

That was yesterday. Today it's not the same, they said.

Together in the Trench

Her eyes are big and black, big and black enough to capture
all the wonder in the world. They look around her in the
night, watch a single star in the infinite sky hurtling down at
the speed of light with a sound like thunder. It drops on the
surface of the earth and explodes like a huge ball of fire,
spreading out into a sea of flames before her eyes. Now she
cannot tell day from night for the fire has gone out and there
are only clouds of black smoke with the sharp smell of dust
creeping up her nose. Under the palm of her right hand is the
feel of her gun and with the feel of her left hand she clasps
his fingers tight. She hears his voice say quietly: You fired
your gun at him and he has fallen to the ground. Look.

She lifted her head over the top of the trench and looked
around but could see nothing. The clouds of smoke were as
dense as night and there was not a single light anywhere. She
could not even see his face. She said, I cannot see, and he
said, Neither can I. So she stared into the darkness for some
time until she glimpsed him in the trench standing by her
side. He still held his finger on the trigger of his gun, and he
still held its muzzle pointing to the sky. He said: One of them
has fallen but there are others still alive. In the darkness she
saw his arm stretch out to her with a piece of folded paper in
his hand. If I die take this letter to my mother.

She whispered: Who is your mother? And he said: My
mother lives close to the orphanage in the House of Joy. She
realized at once that it was Fadl Allah speaking to her, that
he was still alive, that he walked on the earth, his back
straight as a spear, his head raised proudly to the sky. His
skin was brown like river silt, his features pale and fine, and
his eyes look straight into other eyes, their gaze unwavering,
not slipping to one side or dropping to the ground. They

71

shone in wonder like a child seeing the world for the first time and yet their steadiness was that of a man not to be taken by surprise. She said: I am Bint Allah. Can you see me in the dark? And now it dawned on him that all the time he had known that it was her, her face, her eyes, the way she walked, the fragrance of her hair. He said: And Nemat Allah? Nemat Allah died of love. And you? Love for me is life. I do not want to die. She took him in her arms and held him tight. What have you written in your letter? I have written to say that you should not be sad for me, my mother. I have not seen you since I was born, and I have not been to visit you in the House of Joy. But you should not be sad, my mother. Dying for my country means that I have lived for you. So forgive me for this absence which will last forever.

She closed her eyes and said: I see you as though it was only yesterday when you left. I see you as you are, as you always have been. You have never been absent, you have always been with me. He closed his eyes and rested his head on her breast just as he used to do when still a child, then suddenly awakening opened his eyes and looked at her, seeing her as she was now, a woman. They were still in the trench and time had stopped moving. He put his arms around her, and the trench became too narrow for the two of them, too narrow for his arms stretching out to enfold her, too narrow for the vast universe, as vast as the burning disc of the sun up in the heavens. And she too wound her arms around him and the trench was now too narrow for her, for her to hold the universe in her embrace. And when the light revealed them in the trench holding each other, they did not unwind their arms or move apart but held each other in a long embrace, their bodies slowly merging into one and the whole world stood still to watch a scene of love, to see two beings changing into one, never to part again, never afraid of the light, never afraid of death, for each of them had known what dying was. Now he and she were gone, lost in one another, dissolved. Now no force in the world could make them part again, neither the noise of guns and rockets all around nor the loud abuse of enemies or the whispers of their friends, nor the orders of the Imam or the Devil or the Chief of Security himself.

I opened my eyes and found myself standing in the trench alone with the letter folded in my hand. Where was Fadl Allah? I wondered. Where had he disappeared to? Had he died in the war? Had he died in prison? In the distance I could hear their panting breath draw nearer, their feet treading on the ground with the sound of their iron-heeled shoes. So I started to run in the dark of night, trying to save my life. They kept coming after me, their dogs yapping and barking behind them, and I kept on running, not knowing why I was running like this all the time. I had got as far as the spot where the hill begins to rise. It was just before the break of day and I was on the verge of giving them the slip when one of them took aim at me and got me in the back. My body continued to run a few steps, then fell to the ground, but before the letters of the alphabet had disappeared from my mind I said: He was my brother and he was with me in the children's home. Your sins are without end and shall be counted against you, in this world and in the world to come, I heard them say. You are a child of sin and so is he, and his name is not written either on the lists of Hizb Allah or on those of Hizb Al Shaitan.

I was running and the night was black as ever. I could hear them tread with their iron feet as they chased after me. I touched my belly with my hand, feeling for it in the night as I ran. It was round and smooth and loving, warm under my palm. His voice reached me, calling from a distance, sounding like the voice of my mother. Bint Allah, come here. He moved nearer to me, until our bodies almost touched. I wound my arms around him and we locked in a tight embrace. A shiver like a strange fever went right through me deep inside. A voice whispered softly in the night: Fear not, I am God and you shall give birth to Christ. It was dark and I was still running with the letter held tightly in my hand. I hid it in my bosom when I heard them panting close behind. I said to myself, I will not let them touch me before I have delivered his letter to her. I will risk my life to save it. It is more precious to me than the most precious thing I have. I will risk being stoned to death, like the Virgin Mary who risked her life to give birth to her son, like my mother who died to bring me to the world. When I reached the place where the hill starts to rise upwards midway between the river and the sea, the smell of the earth came back to me. Suddenly I felt safe and just at the moment when I could have escaped I stopped to thank God for saving me. As I knelt in prayer they hit me in the back. They always strike me from behind and when I turn around to face them they quickly disappear. They never look me in the face. Before I fell to the ground wounded in the back I said to myself, My belly was full of the fruit of love when I kneeled on the ground to pray, but I hear the Chief of Security say, Love does not exist, only the fruit of sin.

Collective Fear

On the night of the Big Feast while the drums were beating and the pipes were blowing in celebration of victory, they came upon her body where it lay on the way leading from her house to the front, just where the hill starts to climb midway between the river and the sea. She was lying on her back and her eyes wide-open and black looked up at the sky steadfastly. Her face was still and the world was still, as though everything had stopped to look at her there where she lay. Not a hair moved on her head in the night breeze, not a tremor touched the down on the edge of her nose or over her neck. Under the moon her skin which was as brown as silt had turned pure white like that of a maiden in Paradise or a mermaid rising from the sea. Nothing covered her naked body, neither robe nor blouse nor slip. Her nakedness was stark, complete, so revealing of every detail that in death it seemed to speak of sin. For what woman living or dead would go stark naked like that? If she took off her veil, she would still keep her robe, and if she took off her robe she would still keep her blouse, and if she took off everything she would still wear a slip.

But there she lay on her back as naked as a newborn babe with her face looking up at the heavens and her brow like her breast pure and gentle and serene. But her nipple was hard and erect, definitely black, and between her legs was a deep wound, a gash in the flesh which she hid with her hand. At least that was what they said. And since she was hiding her wound it could only mean she had wounded herself. In other words she herself had killed herself. And since it is God alone who gives us life it is God alone who has the right to kill, to take it back. Therefore to kill oneself is to rebel against the will of God. To kill oneself is a crime. But that was not all. Had she not been found completely naked? Her crime was therefore a double crime, that of killing oneself and that of being naked, for nakedness was a crime no doubt. Thus she had committed two crimes, to which they added a third, the crime of being an orphan without father or mother. And now that she was dead nothing was left of her except a name composed of three names kept inside a blue folder in the Security Department with an empty line for her father and an empty line for her grandfather and a line in which was written the third name inherited from her mother. Opposite each of her three names were registered the three crimes she had committed: killing, being an orphan and dying naked.

It was the night of the Big Feast. A whole year had circled round the earth making the Feast of the Sacrifice coincide with the Day of Great Victory and giving the people a double occasion to celebrate. So they gathered under the street lamps and sat cross-legged on the ground pushed up against one another. Their features were grey, their faces thin, the bones of their heads almost bare of flesh, their sharp noses prominent. From openings in their faces they blew out smoke and words, and below the bushy whiskers on their upper lips air moved in and out with a coughing sound. Then gulping down smoke and coughs and words they closed their mouths and were silent for some time. But tiring of the silence after a while they sneezed once or twice, peered at the sky cautiously to make sure that all was well and started to tell stories about kings and gods, and devils and djinns. One of them said: Fellows, remember the good old days when we used to worship the sun and the God of Floods. Another commented: Yes, verily, Allah is witness that the God of Floods gave us no peace until we satisfied him with a virgin girl. He did not like women who were married or widows or women whose husbands had divorced them. Still another said: What a cunning God he was, fellows. A fourth one commented: All Gods were like that. The soldiers used to go searching from one peasant's house to the other looking for a virgin girl to take away. The girls would hide on top of the mud-oven or under the dry fodder or in the buffalo shed. But the God would remain full of wrath until he had been satisfied with the blood of a virgin. Then someone else added: Not even King Shahrayar at his mightiest was like that. A man who had been silent till then said: Why speak only of King Shahrayar. All kings are like that.

Upon which they gulped down their words, their smoke and their saliva with the air, and throwing cautious looks at the door of the Security Department relapsed into a deep silence, with their bodies reclining and their weight carried on their elbows digging a small pit in the ground as the days went by. A column of ants crawled slowly towards the pit misled by their queen leader, for the colour of the elbows made them look as though they were part of the ground on which they rested. But alerted at the last moment that something was wrong and that the elbow could shift its position and squash their bodies, the queen changed her direction and circled round the pointed tip of the elbow where it rested in the hole, and at once the line of ants deviated to one side to make a perfect semicircle before resuming its slow march in a straight line.

The dark pupils of the men fastened themselves intently on the slow columns of ants swarming over the ground like an army. They struck one palm against the other in great amazement as though they were witnessing something extraordinary and sucked at their lips noisily to emphasize the astonishment that had seized hold of them. An army of ants led by a queen, by a female! This was certainly the reason for which God had condemned the ants to crawl over their bellies for all time. They kissed their palms, then the back of their hands, in gratitude to Allah for not having made them ants, though they were never able to advance in a straight line even under threat of a big stick held high in the hand of a guard, and even though their leader was a man and not a woman. They sneezed and coughed, arranged small packs of tobacco neatly under the funnel of their smoking pipes and shifted the weight of their bodies carefully from one elbow to the other. The sound of rockets being fired, the acclamations of the crowds and the lilt of patriotic songs kept echoing in their ears, reminding them that they were supposed to be celebrating both the Feast of the Sacrifice and Victory Day together.

But the year circled round the earth once more and this time they found themselves celebrating the birthday of the Imam on the same day. Thus they had the signal privilege of witnessing three glorious events all being celebrated at the same time, and when they realized all the glory and joy that was theirs, since they were celebrating the Big Feast of the Sacrifice, the Day of Great Victory and the Birthday of their One and Only Imam together, the night seemed to cast its heavy blanket over their eyes. Their lids became heavy with sleep, their hearts became as heavy as stone, and the embers of their smoking pipes went out. They remembered those among them who had died in the war, or who had been lost and had neither died nor returned from where they went. They remembered those among them who had had a left hand and a right foot cut off, the men and women who had been stoned to death, or put in jail and concentration camps. They remembered the mutilated of the war, the martyrs and the handicapped. They remembered those who had died of radiation as they drank their morning milk and those who were alive but were going to a certain death by order of the great Mawlanah.*

They inhaled the last whiff from their pipes as the last shred of tobacco was burnt, and the last ember went out. They swallowed their last words with the bitter taste in their mouths, letting them go down their gullets on an empty stomach preparing to go to bed without food. And just before dropping into a coma-like sleep they discovered that their bodies had not been reclining on their elbows whether right or left, nor had they been held upright by the legs on which they stood, nor been supported by the seats on which they sat, and that in fact they had neither been reclining nor standing nor sitting as they thought but crawling on their bellies, zigzagging from one side to the other unlike ants which tend to move in a straight line, pushing a way through for themselves, making pits with their elbows in each other's bellies as they fought their way with hands and feet. They discovered that each of them kept straining his neck to see what was happening at the beginning of the column, so that

* He who is responsible for the people. The religious leader.

78

his head almost mounted on the head of whoever was in front of him, yet no one could get a glimpse of anything at all because the column extending to where the sky and earth met kept twisting like the spiral of a spring. The black pupils in their eyes were going round and round in a strange panic and noises seemed to mingle in their ears so that they could no longer distinguish between the acclamations of the crowd and the crackling noise of rockets, or between the screams of people and their hallelujahs.

But all of a sudden they opened their eyes and gradually coming back to themselves they realized that it was the Big Feast, and that they were wearing new shoes with iron hooves which made a clinking noise as they walked in the streets. The Imam had decreed that a bonus be distributed to them on this occasion and that at the end of the month their pay be adjusted to the rise in the cost of living. They marched in rows one after the other on their way to acclaim the Leader and as each row passed the tread of their feet could be heard, yet the columns in which they marched continued to waver like a swarm of ants advancing without a queen. Their eyes kept shooting glances around them, looking for God as though they were unable to find Him. Where art thou, O God of the heavens and the earth? And at the spot where the hill starts to rise upwards between the river and the sea, they halted, looked around them as though they had never been to the place before, and a gasp of wonderment could be heard rising from their compact mass, for there she lay on the ground, her back to the earth, her face to the sky, her eyes wide open and densely black. They nodded their turbanned heads and said: There is no God but Allah, praise be to Him. She has died God's death for it is God alone who makes it so that people die. But one of them said: This is not God's death. I know who killed her and the killer is not God.

They were seized with fear and deep inside prayed that God have mercy on them for what the man had said, since no one dies except by the hand of God, and holding their breath they stared at the heavens as though God had a hand that could be seen up there above their heads. But seized once more with fear at this new heresy, for God unlike man hath neither tongue nor hand, they kneeled, bowing their

79

heads low to the ground. Then sitting up cross-legged they moved their heads close together and whispered to one another in hushed tones before lifting their eyes up once more to the heavens in silent prayer: God have mercy on us. After which they all started shouting, Glory to God, to our country and to the Imam. The smallest doubt is a great sin, they said to one another. No one dies except by the will of God. Then crying out in one voice, There is no God but Allah, they buried her deep in the ground.

But her heart continued to beat. Three days her heart continued to beat after she died, they said, and for seven days her spirit wandered around the spot where she lay. Then on the eighth day her spirit left her grave and started to move towards the elevated piece of land between the river and the sea. They swore by God Almighty that they had seen her with their very eyes walking on her own two legs, moving at her usual quick pace with her head held upright and her dog Marzouk behind her. They said however that nobody had been able to look into her face and that they had only seen her from behind, but they swore by Allah, their land and the Imam three times that it was certainly her and nobody else and that her spirit had risen from the grave to take revenge on them, so much so that they were unable to stop themselves from trembling all the time.

Fear dwelt inside them day and night and refused to give them a moment's respite. Nothing was able to keep it away, not even the covers under which they slept, nor the long robes in which they dressed. Fear followed them everywhere, even to the toilet rooms or behind the closed doors of their homes, for they thought she could pass through anything, could see them wherever they went and yet remain invisible herself, so that if one of them slipped out of the bed of his wife to go to that of another woman she would see him, and if a man took off his clothes and remained naked she would see him, and if one of them put his hand in the pocket of another she would see him, and if a man put his hand on his male organ while he slept she would see him. They now feared her just as much as they feared God, and when they slept she appeared to them as God for none of them had the feeling that he was innocent. Each one of them had picked up a stone and thrown it at her. Their lids were heavy with sleep and their hearts were heavy with guilt, and at night when they slept they huddled close up to each other, for they were afraid to sleep alone or to open a door and go out alone in the night.

The only two who escaped this fear were her mother and her dog Marzouk, for neither of them had ever caused her the slightest harm. So her mother continued to wait for her in the dark of the night, standing where she always stood steadfast as a rock, with her hands clasped over her bosom and her face lifted up to the sky. At her feet lay Marzouk curled up like a child, his face pale and thin, and the corners of his eyes seemed to shine as though each of them hid a frozen tear. He held his ears erect, straining himself eagerly to hear her footsteps before she came in sight. His neck was stretched, his nose pointing up to catch her smell amongst the myriad odours of the universe. His eyes were trying to discern the shine of her eyes amongst the myriad stars in the endless heavens and before she had the time to come in sight he ran up to her, lifting himself on his hind legs, reached up like a child for its mother's bosom, then drying his eyes on the tail of her robe, listened to her panting breath as she ran through the night, gazing at the fine thread of blood as it trickled down her body, and at the deep, deep wound in her back.

Eternal Love

He said to her: I will love you forever.

She said: If you want me to believe you, do not say forever.

He said: You must believe that my love for you will last forever.

She said: I beg of you, do not say forever if you wish me to believe that what you say is true.

He said: But I swear to love you with a love which will remain eternally true.

She asked: What do you swear by when you say that your love for me will last forever?

I swear by God, my land and the Imam.

She said: Then I believe you and will put my life completely in your hands. My mind, my heart, my body, make me what I am and in love they are all one for you to have.

In the morning she saw his picture in the paper. It was a big picture and showed him wearing the Medal of Valour on Victory Day. Underneath was a short line announcing his marriage to the daughter of the Chief of Security.

She said: Yesterday you said to me that you love me.

He said: That was yesterday, but today is not the same day as it was yesterday.

She said: Can you betray me and yet remain faithful to your country?

He said: I am not one man. I am two men in one. The man who was with you yesterday is not the man I really am. He was the other man. I am the man who loves you dearly. Love and marriage are two different things and should not be seen as one.

She said: Then you married her without love.

He said: Her father was after me all the time, hunting me down like Satan, so I said to myself to avoid the harm he can do to me the best thing is for me to take the apple of his eye from him. Then he will fall right into my hand and be forced to do what I wish. I needed to possess her and where it is a question of possessing, to speak of love is no longer relevant.

The following night he found her lying in the arms of another man. When he saw the face of this other man he started to tremble all over for the man was no other than the Chief of Security in person.

He said: Do you betray me with another man?

She said: I am not one woman. I am two women in one. The woman who was with you yesterday is not the woman I really am. She is the other woman. I am the woman who loves you, and who will love you for all time. Love and marriage are two different things and should not be looked upon as one.

He asked: Is he your husband?

She said: He kept threatening my father with imprisonment so I said to myself to avoid the harm he can do to us the best thing is for me to marry him as soon as I can. Thus he will fall right into my hands and be at my beck and call. I needed to possess him and where it is a matter of possession, to speak of love becomes irrelevant.

They embraced one another for a long, long while. No one could see them in the silent night. No one could hear them make a silent vow, as they swore by God, by their land and the Imam that their love would last forever. And at the peak of their ecstasy he said to her that according to Shariat a man could have four wives at the same time, but in love he could only love one woman. So she asked him: Are you a member of Hizb Allah or a member of Hizb Al Shaitan? I am a member of both parties, he said. But can a man be a member of two parties at one time? There is nothing in Shariat which prohibits a man from being a member of two parties. Since I believe that God exists and since I believe that Satan exists and since I fear both of them, in order to avoid the harm which can come to me from either of them I decided to join the two parties, said he.

In the quiet of the night he heard her say: You live in eternal fear.

The Great Writer

Rest your hand on my head and do not leave me alone for you are the only person in the world who can sit by my bedside and watch me die, for with you I have no feeling of shame or guilt. If my four wives come to visit me, close the door of my room and do not let them in, for I do not wish to read the hidden satisfaction in their eyes as they see me dying. If a man comes along with a pail of water to wash my body, do not let him in, for when my father died I saw a man like him turn his body over on its face and push one of his fingers up the hole at the end of his back. Since then I decided never to allow anybody to wash my body before burial. I do not understand the sense in washing my body only to bury it in the dust after that. But you know mother, people live their lives and then die without ever using their minds. After the Iman bestowed the title of Great Writer upon me I married a new wife, was provided with a new house and bought the best furniture I could find so that if the Imam visited me one day I should not feel ashamed. Since the day he bestowed the title on me and then decorated me with the Medal of Art and Literature I decided that it would be wrong for me not to be at his side all the time. He said, You must vow always to be loyal to me, then he stood me up in front of him with the Holy Book held in my hand and made me swear eternal loyalty. He said, I am the Imam and no one shall share power with me, and you will be my Great Writer. You shall have a whole page to yourself in the daily newspaper with your picture placed in a frame at the top. Your seat will be separated from mine by one seat only, that of the Chief of Security. But at night nothing at all will come between us as we drink toast after toast in honour of a friendship which has lasted since the days of our childhood.

When I stood beside him in the first row with the lights projected on him from all sides, and the arches celebrating victory raised on all the streets, and with the acclamations of the people echoing like thunder in my ears, I never realized that he could fall down from on high, or die as other men die. I still had a brain in my head but it seemed to have stopped working, why I do not know. I had forgotten how my father had died, how others had died, how the newspapers were full of the names of those who died every day. The thought of death was in my mind, and yet somehow it never occurred to me that I myself would die. As I stood close beside him I heard the sound of bullets being fired, saw him drop down by my side and saw myself drop down by his side, and yet despite all that my mind remained unable to grasp what was happening. I would go on living as though forever. No matter how much I tried to change my mind all my efforts were in vain, and even if at certain fleeting moments I managed to realize that my own life would come to an end, when it came to him I really could not see him dying.

How could he possibly die when his picture looked down on me all the time, was all around me up in the sky, or on the land hanging down from the top of arches or columns or walls or high buildings, or looking out from the pages of daily newspapers morning, noon and night? How could he possibly die when his name was on every mouth, his voice in every call to prayer, his words quoted to define wrong and right, sin and virtue, honour and shame? How could I think of him dying when he continued to stand high up on the elevated platform while the festive rockets burst in the sky, when the words of his speech, slow, stammering in the midst of their flow, were punctuated at every stammer with a roar of acclamation from the crowd?

There I stood listening to him as he stammered his way through, hearing the applause which with every stammer seemed to grow, my mind unthinkingly going back to the days when he sat beside me in school, remembering how whenever the teacher asked him a question he would open his mouth as wide as he could and start stammering, the children in the classroom laughing at the top of their voices, or how he would walk across the courtyard with his hand behind his back, a group of boys following behind him trying to pull it away and uncover the hole he was hiding in his trousers. During examinations he sat beside me and bending down every now and then whispered from under the seat: Say, do you understand anything about all this shit?

I do not know, mother, how it is that the times have moved in such a way that now he is the Imam while I remain a writer of little importance. But as you know those who were last in class used to join the army or the police forces and soon became leaders or presidents, although they really had nothing to show except their smart uniforms and shining stars on their shoulders. I went to Law School and my father addressed me as the Vizir* but I would say to you in a whisper that I hated law, and hated justice, and hated my father too. At that you caught your breath in a gasp of horror, just like the day when you found me standing naked in front of the mirror examining myself. It was the same mirror in which I had glimpsed my father naked in the arms of another woman. Sensing that I was hiding behind the curtain he jumped out of bed and pulled me out by my ear, then threw me on my bed shouting at the top of his voice that I was walking in my sleep. In the morning when we sat down to breakfast you gave me my usual glass of milk but I refused to drink it, so my father beat me and said to me to drink up my milk. When I continued to refuse he caught hold of me and opening my mouth by force poured the milk down my throat. No sooner did he sit down to the table again than I vomited the milk into his plate. You asked me what was wrong with me since I liked my glass of morning milk, to which he said: The boy is ill, I caught him walking in his sleep. He insisted on putting me to bed and started to pour medicine down my throat which tasted as bitter as poison. I told you that my father was trying to kill me so that I should not be able to tell you what I had seen, and you asked me what I meant. But when I was about to speak I caught the look of death in his eyes and my tongue refused to speak.

* Cabinet Minister.

I watched you every day as you continued to wash his clothes, rubbing away at the yellow stains, seeing them with your own eyes, smelling the other woman in them with your own nose, every day washing and cooking, and waiting for him until he came home late at night, and my heart kept getting heavier and heavier all the time. When I looked into your eyes I could see that you knew, knew that something was very wrong in this world of ours, but you kept silent. If you had said something just once, if you had refused to wash the dirt off his trousers stained with the stain of another woman, or if you had gone to another man, then perhaps what was wrong with the world would have been partly righted, or would have become more bearable, and then perhaps within me would have been born the desire for justice or a belief in God, for when I was a child God to me meant justice. I yearned to see you in the arms of a man other than my father. If you had slept in the arms of another man only once then maybe the balance in my world would have been tipped in favour of justice. The teacher of religious catechism read out of the Holy Book and I listened to the words which meant that an eye should be taken for an eye and a tooth for a tooth, that treachery should be answered with treachery and loyalty met with loyalty. The treachery of my father remained grafted to our life and you did nothing to cut it off before it invaded everything. The sin that was being committed against us seemed to grow each time I saw you smile in my father's face.

I kept searching for justice in vain until one day I came upon the boy sitting next to me, his hand held behind his back to cover the hole in his trousers, his head bowed over his desk as though he had been caught in a shameful act. Whenever the teacher asked him a question he would look around in dismay and start to stammer so hard that the sweat poured down his face. When the boys made fun of him he would say at the top of his voice: Where is the justice in this world? All the boys except me can speak without any difficulty. Why has God created only me with this defect? Then he would come close up to me and whisper in my ear: There is no justice, therefore there is no God. God does not exist. And I would whisper back: Yes, if God existed loyalty

would not have been met with treachery, nor would treachery have been met with loyalty. I was only nine years old at
that time and we were both young children in school, yet
what linked us together was a firm belief that God did not
exist, for my readiness to believe in God depended on your
being unfaithful to my father.

My father remained unfaithful to you right up to the end
and I could not understand why you could not answer back.
Then I understood that you were too afraid to do anything
and that every night you wept in your pillow, that every
night you dreamt that you were in bed with another man,
but when the morning came you never dared to live what
you had dreamt. You feared my father just as you had feared
your father before him, but above all you were afraid of
God. I kept saying to you, mother, an eye for an eye, a good
act for a good act, a bad act for a bad act, but you never
paid much attention to me and even when you did try to
listen you failed to understand, and even when you finally
understood you could not bring yourself to act. Day after
day you fell deeper and deeper into a pit of despair, into total
resignation. If you had only fought back against injustice
once, if you had only stood up for your rights once, then I
might have known the meaning of justice and been brought
to believe that God existed. And since you were incapable of
defending your own rights you became incapable of defending the rights of others, of defending my rights. You watched
my father mete out punishment to me unfairly and when the
struggle between us became more and more cruel you took
sides with him. He was always right and I was always wrong
and you always had good reasons not to defend me. If you
had said he was wrong just once, if you had stood up for
what is right only once, then I might have started to know
what justice meant, started to feel that after all there might
be a God worth believing in. Then I could have given loyalty
in return for loyalty.

Instead I became just like you, mother. I even became like
my father, I met good faith with treachery. I betrayed the
woman who was faithful to me and was faithful to the
woman who betrayed me. I ran away from the girl who
loved and wanted me and married the first woman who

spurned my love and refused me so that I could become the Great Writer by decree of the Imam and so that of all the women of the world I could choose to become enamoured of his wife, just as among all the writing of the world I could choose to write what he dictated to me. Perhaps this was a fair way to divide things up between us, mother. He could take possession of the hearts of the people through me, and I could take over the heart of his wife through him. In any case many was the time when he said to me: A woman is a body and apart from that nothing in her appeals to me. As for me, all I could see in her were her eyes blue as the sea. They were there looking at me all the time and even when I looked into the black eyes of my wife they seemed to turn a deep blue and gaze at me. If I took her in my arms her brown body would become soft and smooth and white like the whitest cream and she would hear me whisper at the moment of ecstasy, Katie. Who is this Katie of yours? she would ask angrily and my tongue would be tied for a long moment before I could say: Where did you hear that name? And she would reply immediately: That is the name you whispered when you came with me. Was she your first love O Great Writer? And I caught my tongue just in time before it could say: No she's my last love dear.

For my first love was not called Katie and in fact I can no longer remember her name, nor can I remember what she looked like exactly. All I can remember is that her face was thin and pale, that her skin was dark and marked with scattered patches in some places and that she was a country girl who had come to the city. When she bent down to clean the floor with water in a pail, the sight of her naked thighs made the blood rush to my head, then rush down to my lower belly and collect in the area around the gland of Satan. You used to lock the door of the kitchen on her, mother, and take the key but while you were asleep I used to slip it out of your pocket. When her belly became swollen with child you beat her savagely on her bare feet with a stick made of cane, upon which she confessed that my father was the cause of her pregnancy, so I had nothing to fear. In fact I had seen him take the key from your pocket many a time but said nothing, knowing that you would never listen to me, or that

89

if you listened you would let it pass without saying or doing anything. Little by little I had ceased to talk about such things. I even used to hold back my urine until the morning came instead of going to the toilets in the middle of the night and risk seeing him with another woman. Sometimes it would flow out of me in a slow warm trickle which made my father insist that I was certainly sick since in addition to walking around in my sleep I had now got into the bad habit of wetting my bed. The day I answered back and said that I had seen him with that woman, you did not believe me and instead of standing up for what was right you trembled all over with fear and let him beat me more cruelly than ever before.

Yes mother, if you had done what you should have done just once I might have learnt from you. But my father was able to do as he wished with me and so as the days went by, little by little I became like him, doing the things he did, even stealing the key from your pocket. When he saw me take the key he said nothing, and if I saw him I also said nothing, and the day when the Big Feast was being celebrated her picture came out in the newspapers showing her as she was being stoned to death, big black eyes in a thin pale face staring out at us, arms lifted up to the sky in silent supplication, her knees like her hands wide apart crying out against aggression as they hurled stone after stone at her body, aiming at the brand of Satan right in the centre. The drums were beating for the Big Feast and rockets kept shooting up into the sky in celebration of victory, but in my mouth was a bitter taste of defeat as she looked out at me with her eyes like two holes of black fire burning through the paper.

I stand in the first row under the lights. Nothing stands between me and the throne except the Chief of Security and next to the Chief of Security the Imam himself. In my ears echoes a single shout, God be with you, repeated by a million voices as he stammers slowly through his speech. But I am plunged in silence for my mind keeps straying far away. In my ears I hear the acclamations of the crowd and the sound of shots being fired from a gun, then I see his face fall off his body where he stands tall and upright under the sun, and almost immediately after my face falls down, landing by its

90

side on the ground, and I can see his face look at my face from under the seat, and just as he used to do in school he stammers: Can you make head or tail of all this?

In those days I used to supply him with all the answers to the examinations but now I was at a loss what to say, so I remained lying on the ground with my face buried in the ground pretending not to have heard anything. Slowly a cloud as dark as night crept over the sky hanging over us like a threat of death. My body became rigid like a wall of rock hemming me in, and the sound of shots being fired echoed again and again high above the repeated acclamations of the crowd. I called out to you, mother, just as I used to do when I was a child and you came up to me in the dark like a reassuring light. You leant over me and I could see your face in front of my eyes and I suddenly realized that I had not seen you for twenty years. I moved closer to you, looked up into you face, smoothed away the sleepless nights that had collected around your small eyes and whispered something to you, but you did not answer. I saw myself standing at a distant window looking out over the silent universe and calling out in a clear ringing voice that I had been here before when I was still a child, and that then my heart had been as big as the sun, loving you as much as I loved the fresh morning milk of the cows. But one night I opened my eyes and I saw my father lying in bed shamelessly naked like Satan, and God punished me for opening my eyes since I should have kept them closed and gone on sleeping. Then I no longer loved the fresh morning milk of cows, nor the light of the sun, and the Imam became my closest friend and I began to believe in God and to shout out at the top of my voice like the others, Glory to God, the nation and the Imam.

The Imam in Disguise

Noises continued to resound loudly all around me and the acclamations of the people rose in a mighty shout as I stood high up on the platform delivering my combined Big Feast and Victory speech. My voice echoed in my ears with its familiar tones but I could tell that it was not my voice but the voice of he with whom I shared being the Imam. I could see his face up in the sky suspended from the arches of victory under the powerful lights of the projectors. He kept pulling on the muscles of his face to overcome their rigid immobility, so that his mouth would open in a big smile, big and generous enough to express his love of God and of all His creatures on this earth. I am indeed grateful that I can lie here away from the lights and from the curious eyes of people. Here I can move my arms freely in the air and my heart feels deeply happy at the thought that in so far as my people, the state and the Super-Powers are concerned I continue to be there standing on the platform delivering my Victory Day speech with my supporters in Hizb Allah, my new wife, my Great Writer, my Leader of the Official Opposition and those who support him in Hizb Al Shaitan gathered around me, whereas I am actually lying here on the ground at the same time, my mind at peace, no longer burdened with the worries of state, or with the problems of the foreign debt, or with defeat in war, or the threat of nuclear radiations or other problems of that kind.

This way I can continue to relax on my back, or roll over on my stomach, and if I wish I can even take off my official clothes and dress like an ordinary man, walk alone without any need for the protection of the Chief of Security or of his agents, whether devils or djinns or otherwise. I can saunter along slowly under the shade of the trees, inhale the fresh air deep into my lungs and leave the muscles of my face relaxed, for I am not required to smile or to frown in order to inspire in others the awe that has to go with those who sit on the throne, nor do I need to communicate that feeling of decisiveness expected of the Imam Allah, or exhibit the big smile which speaks of his great love of God, of the nation and of the masses of ordinary citizens over whom he rules. I move my arms up and down freely in the air as I walk along for none of those who happen to see me knows who I am. My body feels light without all my medals and decorations and without the bullet-proof vest which covered my chest and belly from the top to the bottom like one of those chastity belts that women wear.

Nobody in the whole wide world knows who I am, and nobody stops me on the street to talk to me, or kneels down asking for my blessings, or for a raise or a letter of recommendation. My legs move comfortably in my old pair of trousers made of calico, with a tear in the back. I walk around free as the wind, nothing worries me, and I do not fear that someone will recognize me. The muscles of my face are relaxed since it is no longer supposed to inspire awe or express courage or fear, or weakness or strength, or anything at all. Now I know what it means to be imbued with the serenity and happiness of the gods, to be full of confidence that the world can carry on without me and yet at the same time feel that my voice can still be heard broadcast on the radio or through television satellites to the four corners of this world as well as the next world, that my picture continues to flutter on high surrounded by flags on every side and that the acclamations of the crowd continue to reach me from afar as I saunter slowly along enjoying my situation of Imam without actually being the Imam, hearing the acclamations wafted to my ears without having to suffer the strain of their loud noise.

A small distance away he glimpsed a shadow moving on the shore of the river. At first he thought it was one of those members of Hizb Al Shaitan who had recognized him and was lurking there to kill him. He had always had a fear that someone would penetrate his disguise and discover he was

93

the Imam, although he was even more afraid of being recognized without his disguise. So he quickly hid behind a tree, almost panting with fear, and fastening his frightened eyes on the shadow he watched it carefully for some time waiting to see what it might do. At the beginning it looked like a rock since it seemed to rise up from the ground without showing the slightest movement. But when he looked at it more closely he detected what seemed to be a slight movement, as though the rock was rolling on itself very slowly. He kept his eyes fixed on it to make sure that what he had seen was not an illusion and after a little while noticed that the rock was held up by what looked like four columns and for a moment he imagined it was a buffalo moving along the shore of the river, but then he realized that it had no horns and that its head was surrounded by something which resembled a white turban, so it occurred to him that it was probably an old man kneeling on his hands and knees to implore the Imam. At this thought he felt at ease for the man was surely a member of Hizb Allah and did not represent any danger, so he moved out from behind the tree where he had been hiding and approached, but when he got nearer he realized that it was a woman and not a man and as soon as he saw her he knew who she was.

She was digging deep down into the ground and was so absorbed that she did not feel him as he drew nearer, so he took advantage of this to try to find out what she was doing before she discovered his presence. He saw her smooth out the ground with the palm of her hand, brushing away the stones and pebbles, then cover the ground with soft earth before she wrenched a small bundle away from her breast and laid it down into the pit she had made, making a place for it with the tips of her fingers before she proceeded to flatten the earth around it and shovel handfuls of fine dust to cover it up. He said to himself, she must be one of the slaves of the land whose husband died in the war or in an epidemic. He moved up closer to where she stood, greeted her and after praising her for her labours enquired of her what it was that she had planted. A hazelnut tree, she said. But knowing that a hazelnut tree does not bear fruit before a hundred years have passed, he said: I wish you good health but do you expect to taste the fruits of this tree? She had not lifted her eyes to look at him when he spoke to her but she realized immediately that he was the Imam. I shall not live to see it grow, she said. Then why make all this effort to plant a tree? I am continuing the efforts which others have made before me, she said. It was not I who started to plant but my mother and were it not for her I would not have lived.

He almost said, It was I who gave you life and not your mother, were it not for the fact that he was wearing his disguise and did not want her to know who he was. He controlled his desire to reveal his authority, thinking that it was better if he kept the information to himself so that he could find out whether she was in Hizb Allah or Hizb Al Shaitan. After that I can leave her in the hands of the Chief of Security, he said to himself. So he coaxed the muscles of his face into a smile and, speaking in a gentle voice as though addressing a child, said: Are you in Hizb Allah or in Hizb Al Shaitan? She remained silent, neither saying anything nor raising her eyes to his face. It occurred to him that she must be a member of Hizb Allah and was afraid to reveal the fact to him lest he be the Devil in person or at least one of the evil spirits. She continued to remain silent and he began to suspect that she was trying to be cunning and thus without realizing it had exposed her true self so that before much time passed he would find out what it was that she was trying to hide. His eyes kept examining her closely but he was unable to find anything to indicate that she was really as cunning and wily as he first thought, for on the contrary her face looked as innocent as a newborn child.

And yet the more innocent she looked the more he began to feel that her innocence hid something behind it and that she was without doubt a dangerous female and what was more a child of sin. So he went on playing a game with her, handing her the branch of a tree and saying in his sweetest voice: Take your time girl, for there is no need for you to fear anything even if you happen to be a member of Hizb Al Shaitan, since it also was created by decree of the Imam exactly like Hizb Allah, and do not think that I am trying to find out about you in order to do you harm, for God forbid, that is not my intention at all. On the contrary I want to reward you for the work you have done, and for the efforts you have made without even seeking anything in return. Such behaviour is the very essence of true self-sacrifice as expected by God, our nation and the Imam.

But the woman continued to be silent, her face expressing an even greater innocence, her heart swelling with a pride and happiness so overwhelming that she could hardly contain it. She lifted her eyes and looked up at him. This was the first time she had ever seen him and he looked a strange man, completely bald with not a single hair on his head, but with a face covered in hair and thick eyebrows meeting in a line above his nose. On his forehead was a patch of dark scaly skin like a mulberry and his nose was hook-like, overhanging the big mouth which was twisted to one side. His chin was pointed, with a deep cleft in the middle from which hung down strands of straggly hair like a goat's beard. She told herself that this face looked like that of the Imam, the one she had seen many times in pictures of him, then she thought it could not be possible, for the Imam would surely not be walking around just like other people, nor would he have that big hole in his trousers.

She continued not to say a word and the Imam asked her why she was so silent. I thought you were the Imam but you are not him, she said. And somehow at that point his intelligence seemed to grow sharper and he remembered that information had become an important weapon these days, and he said to himself, Now it is possible for me to test how loyal she is to me and to her country and how great her faith is in God, and so reach right to the bottom of her heart. And he was filled with a great exuberance at the thought that he was now going to probe deep into her heart, whereas neither the Chief of Security nor the Super-Powers had as yet discovered a means to spy on people's hearts. He was so excited with the idea that he started to imagine that he was God in person, forgetting he was only the Imam in disguise, since it was God alone who could get into people's hearts, and he was almost on the verge of revealing his true identity when at the last moment he decided it was better to remain incognito in order to discover her true feelings and how devoted she was to God, to her country and to the Imam. He

96

made a special effort to hide the coarse tones of his normal voice, speaking very gently and taking good care to expose the big hole at the back of his trousers, for the more he hid his real identity the more certain he became that she would reveal the truth about herself, and the things she hid deep in her heart.

He was still standing in front of her when suddenly he noticed that he was very afraid and that his whole body was shaking with fear. He could not understand why it was that he was shaking so, but after a while he started to realize from her continued silence and the steady look in her eyes as she stood facing him that she indeed believed not in God, or in the nation, or in the Imam, that she was not a member either of Hizb Allah or of Hizb Al Shaitan, that she was certainly a devil of a girl and the daughter of a devil of a woman and that both of them had been born in sin. Having reached these conclusions, he said to himself, Now if this is true she is capable of committing the worst sins and the most terrible crimes and there is nothing else that can be done to deal with this than to stone her until she drops dead.

The Philosopher

There is a strange enchantment in this other world which attracts me to it. My old sweetheart Katie fled over there and I have heard many tales and myths like those of *The Thousand and One Nights* about it. I have heard about lust in the eyes and molten gold in the earth, yet here I am in a room without heating. I change from one train to another under the ground. I work as a small employee in a small company and I wanted to marry the daughter of the director. I fell in love with her but she turned me down and so I married a woman whom others had turned down before I met her. She is ten years older than myself and she has a flat chest, thighs thin as walking sticks and no haunches. Her mind is hot and seething with things but her womb is freezing. She gives birth to one book after the other but when it comes to children she prefers test-tube babies. I said to her: To my mind a great woman is the woman who gives birth to a great man not to a great book. She said: The Virgin Mary gave birth to Jesus Christ, but I lost my virginity when I was a child and no longer believed in Christ. I asked: What do you believe in then? I believe in my mind and in anyone who can relate to my mind but not to my uterus, she said.

So I said to myself, I pray that God and Jesus Christ will be my compensation in life, and every morning I rush through the corridors of the underground to ride in long narrow trains like the tubes of test-tube babies, standing in row after row with the other rows, all packed like sardines with the feel of oil and salty sweat around me, or on the escalators closing my eyes and letting myself be carried up to where the cold wind buffets me about as I dash over the pavement shielding myself from the rain with an old black umbrella. When I enter my office I shake the rain off my coat

98

like a sick dog and comb my hair slowly in the mirror. My telephone no longer brings me the tones of a voice I am waiting to hear. All I can expect is the director saying the same things he says every day. This report is urgent, this letter is important, where is the file, I want twenty copies of this document, call the number I gave you again, reserve me a place in the plane, write the memorandum in time for the meeting tomorrow. It never stops ringing and his voice never stops asking and my fingers move over the keys of their own accord as though they are no longer part of me, and time passes with the tick of the clock to bring nothing, no love, no friendship, no hope, not even some fuel for heating. Even despair has gone too.

The walls of my heart are made of white ice. The cup of coffee in my hand is cold and my room is painted a dark grey tinged with a pale blue so that I seem to live in shadow. I have not renewed its paint for the last twenty years. I saved up some money and decided to paint it before last Christmas, but Christmas came and went and I did nothing. They sent rockets under cover of night and with a nuclear war no walls will be left standing, so what use is it painting anew? The walls of my room have no pictures hanging on them, not even a picture of my father or my mother, but in my mind I have an image of my father in his military uniform for that is how my grandmother described him to me. After the end of the First World War he carried me away over the seas and our ship anchored near a mountain of ice. He left me here with his mother and went off to another war. He died without telling me how I was born, and my grandmother knew nothing about his life at all. If I asked her, she would say you looked a handsome baby through the glass of the test-tube, and in my sleep I used to dream of myself swimming in a test-tube looking for my mother when suddenly a huge whale swallowed me up in one gulp, and a moment later I would wake up bathed in sweat.

The tips of his fingers feel icy as they hold the glass. Black coffee without milk every day for breakfast, swallowed without appetite on an empty stomach. An appetite for food, an appetite for love, an appetite for books, are things he knew at one time, but now they are gone. All he reads is the main heading of the first page in the morning newspaper, for he is waiting for a single item of news, a short sentence composed of three words. Nuclear War Declared.

It is five minutes to nine. I pull the covers over my head again. Every day I decide to stay in bed. Every day I say to myself, why get up?, for outside my room there is nothing else but the tarmac street, the rain pelting down, the tunnels under the ground, the trains like the test-tubes with teeming human embryos, the escalators to which I abandon myself as they climb, the keys which my fingers touch all the time, and the voice of the director squeaking on the line. I want an urgent report, this letter is important, write that down, no the other file, a non-smoking seat in first class please and don't forget that I cannot fly otherwise. He smokes but does not like to inhale the smoke of other people's cigars.

One night he invited me to dinner. He said he admired my intelligence, but while we ate his eyes kept running over my body all the time. After we had finished our meal we sat on the sofa eating chocolates and drinking fine champagne cognac. Suddenly he put his arms around me, but I turned my face the other way for his breath smelt. I expressed my appreciation for his wonderful feelings but told him quite frankly that I was very much enamoured of somebody else. Man or woman? he enquired. You have no right to question me about my private life. What do you care whom it is that I love, since it is not you? said I. I left his flat and walked out without even saying thank you or good night. Yet the truth of the matter was that I loved no one, that I was completely free, free of a need to love, of a need to wait for somebody, of a need to hear promises made that were not real. My body was my own, and I had no desire to possess the body of somebody else. All I needed at the time was a sum of money each month to pay the rent, and buy myself coffee and bread, and if I lost my job it meant I would no longer have even that, so next day when he put his arms around me again I whispered words of endearment in his ear. He looked at me and asked if I was all right and told me that my face had changed since yesterday. I explained that in fact I was not feeling too well, that my mouth had a bitter taste like that of black coffee. Have you been to a psychiatrist recently? he

100

said, looking at me in a queer way, and when I answered no, he told me it was better to go since the signs I was showing were most probably those of depression.

The psychiatrist asked me about my life and I told him everything very frankly. So he said to me: The only treatment for you my friend is to travel. What you need is the warmth of love, the rays of the sun and the feel of money in your pocket. So I prepared my bags and when I was ready told my wife that I had decided to travel. Where to? she asked me, and I pointed with the tip of my finger to a place on the map. She put on her spectacles which were thick and green like the bottom of an empty bottle of beer and looked at the place I had pointed to. So that's where you're going, she said, overseas. Don't worry, I said, I will be back very soon carrying diamonds and jewels for you. I kissed her tenderly on a mouth without lips and went off alone thinking of my old love and the new life which waited for me. My heart beat to the chink of gold, and when I looked at myself in the mirror I saw myself living like King Shahrayar raping a virgin each night and killing her at dawn.

From where I was high up in the air I could see the land shining under the sun like liquid gold with a green hill rising in its midst between the river and the sea. The plane landed after sunset and as I stepped out my nose inhaled a smell of things from bygone ages, an odour of sweat mingled with fat and burning kerosene. The air was filled with smoke, from which emerged the grey faces of people, words spoken in an unknown language, lack-lustre eyes staring at me, square bodies wrapped around in cloaks, and children with grown-up faces and swarms of flies devouring their eyes. As I walked out of the airport men wearing long robes gathered around me, almost assaulting me, pulling at my arms now to one side, now to the other, as they quarrelled over my bags. One of them threw me into the taxi-cab and my bags were thrown in after me. The taxi-cab leapt forwards in the dark, surrounded on all sides by the blare of horns and by what seemed to me like rockets bursting in the sky or artillery guns being fired in a continuous barrage. When we were stopped at a crossing by the red traffic lights children rushed up on all sides carrying yellow dusters and started to wipe the front window of the cab vigorously, then they pushed their cracked palms under my nose, but the driver drove them away with angry shouts.

I reached the hotel in a state of collapse and asked the reception if anybody had called me, but they said no. I am waiting for an appointment with the Imam, I said. Today is the Big Feast, and the Imam is in the middle of his speech and everybody else is on holiday, they said. What can I do until the holiday is over? I asked. There is nothing you can do, they said. Everything is closed. But isn't there anything I can see these days? You can go and see the Virgin Mary if you want. She has appeared several times during the last days in the old church neighbouring the new mosque and all the people are gathered to try to get a glimpse of her. And before I had time to decide for myself one of them threw me into another taxi-cab and I found myself seated on the edge of the back seat making the sign of the cross for the Father, the Son and the Holy Ghost.

When I arrived I could hardly believe my eyes. People seemed to have come from the most distant parts of the land and they were there in huge numbers, whether men, women or children, young or old. They were squatting on the ground or sitting on straw chairs, some wearing the peasant robe and others dressed like city-dwellers. There were women with their faces covered in veils and others who walked about showing off their half-naked bodies. There were people who looked ill and hungry and pale, and others with ruddy complexions full of health and vitality. But all of them had their eyes fixed on the dome of the church waiting for the Virgin to appear. They had read about her in the newspapers and all those who had not seen her when she appeared the previous year had come to get a glimpse of her this time. Even the foreigners had come to witness the miracle and they could be seen watching with the others, standing slightly apart, each one with his black dog on a leash squatting obediently on its haunches with its eyes raised reverently upwards to the sky.

A man whispered in his neighbour's ear: Do you think that faith can enter the heart of a dog? And his neighbour

102

answered, Why not? Another man commented: Verily if a dog knows what it means to be faithful to his master, why should he not be led to believe in God, especially dogs like these which are of the very best breed imported from abroad? God has given them the ability to know who is guilty of crime, and who is innocent, and it is known that they feed on whale liver and smile when their picture is taken. The second man who had spoken joined in again, saying: You know their countries are not like our countries and their dogs are not like our dogs. They are the Great Powers, God protect us from their evil, and they send death to us in tins of food, and rockets to raze our cities to the ground, and planes which travel to the moon.

The first man to speak was following what was being said intently and opening his eyes in astonishment exclaimed, To the moon! He looked up at the moon and there it was hanging in the sky without columns or anything else to hold it up. He felt reassured. Yes, God was much greater than the Great Powers. He reigns high above all men and all things in this world. You say they have men who have gone to the moon? Yes, I swear by God that this is indeed true. They have even sent a woman too. The first man looked even more astounded than he did before and broke in again, repeating, A woman?! And the man who had been talking nodded his head with the air of someone who knows all about it and said: I swear by God that it is true, and that they have truly sent a woman. But the first man remained sceptical. A woman, he said scornfully. Tell us what she looked like. Did she have two breasts like our women here, like your wife and my wife? And did she travel alone without her man, without a male companion?* And the second man said she went alone, completely alone, without any male companion and she didn't even wear a veil since there are no men on the moon. Yes there are definitely no men on the moon and even if there are men they are different to men on the earth and are not attracted to the charms of women. The astonishment

* Muslim traditional custom ordains that when a woman travels she must be accompanied by a male companion such as her father, her brother, her husband or some other close male relative.

of the first man now knew no bounds. But if they are not attracted by the charms of women, what is it that attracts them then? God only knows, said the other man. God alone knows what it is that can attract them.

And now they were in the middle of the night and the Virgin had not made her appearance yet. Why had she not appeared? they wondered. Had she changed her mind and decided to show herself in some other land? In the past she had always chosen to appear in this land and if she did not choose their land what other land could she possibly choose? Maybe because they did not believe that Christ was her son she had decided to move somewhere else. And yet she had made an appearance yesterday at the church, so all this did not make any sense. Besides it was known that she made no difference between those who believed in Mohamed and those who believed in the Christ, that she was opposed to sectarian strife. In the newspapers they had described how she came down from the sky and had even published pictures of her dropping on the dome of the church from on high. Don't you read the newspapers? said the first man with a note of impatience. No, I don't know how to read, said the second man pulling at his sleeve. But isn't the Virgin Mary a spirit without body or flesh? She is the purest and most chaste in this world and the next, said the first man solemnly. But do newspapers publish the pictures of spirits without flesh? asked the second man, dropping his voice to a whisper which could hardly be heard. The first man threw him a keen glance and said, Why not brother? They are the newspapers of the Imam and nothing is impossible for them.

A child suffering from paralysis who had been brought by her mother and was sitting there looking up at the sky suddenly cried out and stood up raising her hands to heaven, and immediately all the people gathered around rose to their feet glorifying the name of Almighty God and the Virgin Mary. The two men who had been squatting on the ground talking stood up and started to cry out with the others. After that there was a silence. The first man whispered in the ear of the second man, Is it the Virgin Mary?, and the second man shouted out, Of course, don't you see her up there? So he looked upwards to the dome of the church in the same

104

direction as the others were looking and started to tremble all over because he could see nothing and for a moment he thought he was blind, but then he made a great effort to chase away all doubts and staring into the dark night started to shout with the others, There she is, there she is, as he pointed out with his outstretched hand to the sky.

The Imam nodded his head in great satisfaction and said: This is an excellent project and will change the expanses of desert sand into a real Paradise of Eden. He gave me the title of expert, presented me with a private beach that looked out at the sea, and after that all I had to do was to sign my name on the contract. But before I signed they asked me: What is your name? And I said, Joseph. They said that the origin of Joseph was Youssef and that I would have to change my name. So I said, No harm in that, God and the Lord Jesus Christ will recompense me for sacrificing my name. But then they asked me whether I believed in Jesus Christ and not in the Prophet Mohamed, to which I replied that what mattered most were the interests of the project and that I was prepared to give up Jesus Christ if this was necessary.

After that they enquired about my mother and wanted to know her name, so I had to tell them that I was a test-tube baby and did not know my mother's name. After a moment's silence they asked me what test-tubes were and I explained that test-tubes were a new kind of womb which produced babies completely innocent of any kind of sin since they did not require sex, or marriage, or intercourse between a man and a woman to be born. All that was required was artificial insemination of the egg. This caused a good deal of consternation and they cried out in a loud voice, God protect us from the Devil and his machinations for this is verily the worst kind of adultery and fornication and can only lead to confusion by preventing fathers from knowing their real children. But, said I, what wrong did I commit that you should condemn me like this? I was an embryo in a test-tube womb and knew nothing about adultery or sin or fornication. The only salvation for you, they said, is to purify yourself from sin and declare you faith in the one and only Allah and in His Prophet Mohamed. But how do I purify myself from sin? I asked. It is very simple, they said, all you have to do is to cut off the foreskin that covers your male organ. But at that I broke down and almost on the verge of tears cried out, I can bear anything except to have a part of my body taken away from me. But they insisted that this was the only way I could be purified from my sins, enjoy God's blessings and ensure the success of the project. So at last I gave in, saying to myself, I can undergo purification and lose my foreskin for all this means nothing if the gold starts to roll in.

The barber came, carrying his small bag with him. He purified me by cutting off my foreskin with a razor and the only anaesthetic used in the operation was a bottle of gin which I swallowed down quickly before he had time to begin. When it was over I found that scores of children had gathered round for the same thing and that I was the only grown-up to be circumcised among them. So I lowered my face to the ground in shame and arranged to have my conversion to the faith of Allah published in all the newspapers next day, so that from then on I was known as the Expert Believer and my picture appeared regularly on the front page set in a frame with some declaration or other of mine, as though what I said was considered as setting the line in matters related to the faith. I had answers to every question and solutions to every problem and as time passed I discovered that the whole matter was very simple since all we needed in the final analysis was a return to religion and an unlimited belief in God and His Prophet Mohamed. They would ask me: And now Expert Believer, what do you think of the dangers of nuclear radiations, and what can we do to protect ourselves from them? Pray five times each day and fast the month of Ramadan, I would say. Then they would ask how we could face the rise in the cost of living and the problem of hunger which was increasing rapidly, and I would say, By cutting off the hand of those who steal and obliging women to wear a veil. A short while after that the Imam bestowed upon me the title of philosopher, and God multiplied my gains to the extent that at the end of my contract I packed my bags full of gold and smuggled them through customs without paying duties and escaped in a plane with my old sweetheart Katie.

My Old Love

From the rose-coloured windows of the harem tinted like the setting sun I looked out over the expanse of land between the river and the sea now so vast that it extended as far as I could see, an ocean of undulating green. Across the river was the mosque lying in the low land behind the hill and next to it the home for orphaned children. Further back I could glimpse the Floating Theatre and some distance away the House of Joy buried in a pit behind an area of waste land used as a refuse dump, and between the two the military hospital with big glass windows shining in the light. Behind the windows stood the army doctors laughing and whistling to the girls in the Nurses' Home, lifting their military caps off their heads and waving them in the air. In their hands they carried children's guns with which they shot down the birds standing on the branches of the trees. They kept pulling crackers out of their pockets, blowing on them with their breath to warm them up and then throwing them on the ground to explode suddenly with loud noises which mingled with the acclamations of the crowd celebrating the Big Feast and the sound of rockets shooting to the sky.

The Imam could be heard delivering his speech and I stood listening with the others in the balcony reserved for the harem, surrounded by baskets of roses and dancing groups of children dressed like white angels, while the women of the charitable societies stood on either side of me dressed like black crows, clapping their hands in applause every time the Imam stammered and stuttered through a few words. Behind me in close rows were the model mothers, widows of martyrs and the martyred men and women of the war. The Imam stood high up on the elevated platform with his arms lifted to God and the acclamations of the crowd resounded like shots fired from a gun, and suddenly his rubber face fell down and landed between his feet so he hid it in the ground. And when I saw what happened I buried my face in my hands and prayed to God and His Prophet that the earth might swallow me up and make me disappear off its surface. Then I prayed to the Lord Christ and his mother the Virgin Mary that I be transformed into a spirit which could fly up in the air without being seen by the eyes of human beings. If I could only go back to my mother and take refuge once again in her womb!

I imagined her waiting for me at the door with her arms held out to me as I ran up the stairs of the old house. She hugs me tightly and whispers in my ear: Why have you been so late in coming my dear? Where were you all this time? she asks. With a stranger over the sea. But why, my child, why give your life to a stranger who is not from here? He had a throne with many servants and women slaves, and I was tired of washing plates and of smiling into faces that never smiled at me. I was tired of being the daugher of a man who refused to recognize me. And my mother said: But washing plates is much simpler than washing the body of a man after he is deceased, and to be recognized by one's mother is worth much more than a father's seal.

I leave her standing there and run down the old pathway. At the end next to the church is a small house and as I knock at the door I can feel my heart beat against my ribs until the door opens to reveal a face I know so well that I can never mistake it for another face. It is the face of Lord Jesus and he too knows me so well that as soon as he opens the door he recognizes me, takes me into his arms and says: Why have you been so long in coming my dear? Where have you been? And I say: I was with my husband the Imam overseas. Do you betray me with that husband of yours Katie? he says. I have never betrayed you Joseph, I say, for when I am with him I love you more every day. When I hold him in my arms I close my eyes and imagine that you are so near to me. He said: You have always been my only love and after you left me I have only loved men or women without breasts who give birth to books instead of children. When I closed my

108

eyes to go to sleep I prayed that love would come to me, but instead what used to come was a coma-like state which brings forgetfulness and losss of memory, but keeps the eyes wide open, a heavy sleep like death which keeps the mind awake remembering, so that I am unable to forget you, or the Lord Messiah, or my name, or my body when it was whole without a wound. I asked, What wound? But he holds me in his arms silent as a tomb.

And when I look into the round mirror hanging above the bed I see the Imam holding me tight in his arms, and instead of one man there are now a hundred men all holding me in their embrace, so I hold him in my arms as though I am giving myself to all the men in the world, and my hand creeps down under his trousers to touch his wound where it hurts him after they made him pure, and it smells like dry old wood, and I say to him: At one time you smelt green like the newborn branch of a tree. That was in the days when you used to love me, he said, but then you left me to go and look for gold, and so I followed you and did the same as you did. I embraced him in the mirrors and wiped away my sweat with a scented handkerchief, and he sniffed and said: Have you changed your scent? No, I said, but my body has lost the odour of childhood. I rested my head on the back of the bed, then put a pillow behind my head and the smell was in my body although I kept washing it with scent, like an odour of death which hung around and would not leave me. He said: Do not think of that. I love you better on the throne even though your youth has fled. Do not try to change yourself, to hide your age or the wrinkles in your face. The glass trembled in my hand and spilt my drink on the bed and I laughed like a child that had spilt its milk, but on the sheet the stain was dark and never went no matter how much I tried to wash it off or bleach it white.

As I lay on the bed my body felt flabby and I had to make an effort to lift its weight and get out of bed so that I could go to my place on the royal seat. I hid it behind a huge desk, seeking refuge in books and various papers. My name was etched in silver letters on a book I never opened and the name of my husband was printed in gold on a book he had never written. He came in smelling of drink and sweat from the other woman but I looked up at him and said nothing for I was not the only woman in his life nor was he the only man I had known. In him I sought refuge from poverty and in me he sought comfort in defeat. Deep inside my soul is the bitterness of knowing the truth and on all sides I am besieged by the death of illusion. I can feel dust filling my nose as I look around for the throne which has disappeared, but I can see the Imam stretching out his arms trying to hold me, so I stretch out my arms and try to cling on to him, but the closer our bodies approach the greater the distance between us grows, so that at the moment when we touch each other and hold one another close we are furthest away. It has always been so, for since the first day we embraced we were distances away and no matter how much we tried to be close it has always been in vain.

I liked to read in my soft bed before going to sleep but he would move up to me, sitting on his haunches with a glass in his hand and start telling me what had happened during the day. He would say something, then I would say something, and so we would go on talking, not without pleasure in conversing together. But as soon as he put his arms around me all the pleasure would disappear in a moment. I preferred hearing him talk to feeling his arms circle themselves around me. A dialogue between our two bodies was never set up right from the beginning, as though they spoke two different languages. When we talked I could understand him and he could understand me and each of us gave and took. But when we embraced the balance seemed to tip, to be replaced by a single movement on his side where there was always sudden attack and sudden retreat, as though pleasure was a sin and a lust, a weight which he carried around desiring to be rid of it as fast as he could.

In the mirror I would see him as he lay in bed, watch him as he became two men, one the Imam and the other an exact double or copy of the Imam. I would often see him walking along the corridors of the palace with his Body Guard near him, and at night when he embraced me I became confused and asked him many a time whether he was the Imam or the Body Guard, and he would answer quickly, I am the Imam. He resembles you so closely that sometimes I cannot tell the original man from the copy. I am more powerful than he is in mind, and he is more powerful in body than I am, and as time goes by my mind gets bigger and my body grows weaker, and you are young enough to be my daughter so that sometimes I am afraid that one day I will come back from one of my trips like Shahrayar to find you in bed with my Body Guard. I asked, Who is Shahrayar? and he said, Have you never heard of Shahrayar, have you never read *The Thousand and One Nights*? No, I said. Then you haven't studied our cultural heritage and you should make up for that by reading, he said. He got out of bed and slowly walked up to the library, then stood in front of it for a long time reading the titles of the books with difficulty. From the slight bend in his shoulders I could tell it was the Imam and not the Body Guard, and at the same time I realized that I knew him better from the back, which gave me a shock not devoid of a certain pleasure, for understanding even if painful is better than ignoring the facts. After all it is certainly better for me to know him from the back rather than not to know him at all. I walked up to him on the tip of my toes and put my arms around him from behind, for I loved him more from the back than from the front and I loved him best when he was completely absent.

He turned round and came back from the library carrying a huge book in his hands with an effort. He steadied his spectacles on his nose and I could see the gold chains attaching them to his ears dangling down on either side. As he read, his eyelids would close heavy with sleep but his mouth remained half-open reciting the verse of the Seat in order to chase away devils and evil spirits, and he held the book in his arms as one would hold the woman one loves. In the dark he stole out of bed and went to her, and from where I hid I could see him clasp her in a warm embrace, and although to see her in his arms was painful to my heart, yet it was better than my not seeing what was going on. The feeling of knowing, of discovering, was like tasting a forbidden pleasure, something one did in secret on one's own, and I had no jealousy or anger in my heart when I saw him, only a feeling of guilt as though I was being more unfaithful to him than he was being to me, for the truth was that I was enjoying his love-making to her more than I enjoyed his love-making to me.

Reviving Our Cultural Heritage

I was alway very interested in our cultural heritage and before I went to sleep enjoyed reading one of the books that were a part of it. The book which I enjoyed best of all was *The Thousand and One Nights*. Before reading I would take off the face of the Imam and put on my spectacles. In the mirror I saw a face that was round and under the light my complexion and my teeth became white and shining like those of King Shahrayar. My heart was like his, white and pure, imbued with a great love for black slave women. My soul like his soul was innocent and could not understand how a woman could love a man other than the husband she had married. My body trembled in agony at the thought of Shahrayar's wife in bed with his black slave and at night I would dream of my wife sleeping in the arms of one of my black slaves and would suddenly wake up with wide-open eyes to find her sleeping alone in her bed with her book in her arms and her eyes tightly closed. My mind tranquil and my heart at rest I felt a wave of confidence sweep through me and after a short while I slipped out of bed, careful not to make any noise, and in the dark of night went to my black slave. On my way to her just like King Shahrayar.

I stopped under a tree to breathe in the fresh air and enjoy the feeling of going out alone, without a guard and completely unknown to those who might see me. There I stood taking deep breaths of fresh air when I noticed a gigantic man carrying a box on his head pass by. I thought he must be an evil spirit or one of my enemies from Hizb Al Shaitan and was so alarmed that I quickly climbed up the tree and hid in its branches, just as I used to do when I was still a young child. He put down the box and sat on the ground under the tree, rested for a moment and then started to open the locks with which the box was closed, one lock after the other until he had opened seven locks. Inside the box was another box which opened and out came a woman. She was a very beautiful woman and I heard the man say to her, My darling devoted wife I want to sleep for a while, then he put his head on her knees and immediately fell asleep. The woman lifted her face upwards to the tree where I was hiding and whispered in a soft voice: Come down and fear nothing for this devil sleeping on my knee is not a spirit but an ordinary man. As soon as I had climbed down from the tree she moved his head off her lap and rested it on the ground and then did with me exactly as a woman does with her husband, and the things which happened to me were all that a virtuous man could possibly hope for if he found himself alone with a nymph from Paradise. But before I took leave of her she pulled a small bag out of her pocket and extracted from it a necklace of ninety-nine rings, saying to me, Do you know what this is? I have no idea, said I. The owners of these rings, said she, are the men with whom I did what I did with you just now, but my husband has never found out. She asked me for my ring and when she had threaded it on to the necklace, pointed to her husband and said: This man kidnapped me on my wedding night and hid me in a box which he put inside another box, then locked it with seven locks and buried me under the ground, not knowing that if a woman wants to do something there is nothing in the world that can stop her.

My body started to tremble all over and I felt my heart drop. So I took leave of her and ran back to the palace as fast as I could, only to find my wife in bed with her lover. So I cut off her head with my sword exactly as King Shahrayar had done before and then went off to my older wives and cut off their heads with the same sword one after the other. Now every month when the moon was full I married a virgin, took away her chastity and after that cut off her head with a sword. I went on doing the same thing for twenty years until people could stand it no more and their daughters abandoned their homes and ran away, so that the day came when there remained not a single girl who could be taken to bed. So on the night of the Big Feast I called in my Chief of Security and

113

told him that I was looking for a slave girl who was a virgin and that she should be the most beautiful thing ever seen in our times. And to make sure that what I wanted was clear I read out a list of qualities I desired in this maiden, taken straight from the cultural heritage which I had always held in high esteem. I said that I wanted her to be slender of waist, opulent of breast, with dense black eyelashes, a small head and large buttocks, her breath smelling like the scent of flowers in a garden, skilful in the art of love, and never touched by any man before. I wanted four things in her to be a white as milk, her face, the parting of her hair, her teeth and the white of her eyes; four things in her to be as black as night, her eyelashes, her eyebrows, her eyes and her hair; four things to be rosy-red, her tongue, her lips, her cheeks and the flesh under her white skin; four parts to be well-rounded, her legs, her wrists, her haunches and her belly; four parts to be large, her brow, her forehead, her eyes and her breasts; four parts to be small, her mouth, her nose, the openings of her ears and that other hole which is sought after in women more than anything.

The Chief of Security listened without saying a word and by the time the Imam had finished listing what he wanted he was as pale as death. For the first time in his life he felt inclined to believe in reincarnation, saying to himself, Indeed this must be the spirit of Shahrayar which has come to inhabit the body of the Imam or else the spirit of the Imam which has lived in the body of Shahrayar. He remained silent, his head bent to the ground as the words of the Imam echoed in his ears describing his needs, ticking them off on his fingers lest he forget anything until he reached the four things which he wanted to be small: her mouth, her nose, the openings of her ears and that other opening which is sought after in women more than anything. Then raising his head at last, he said: But Lord Imam, such a slave as you describe cannot be found for less than ninety thousand dinars and the Treasury of the State is empty, that is apart from our foreign debts. . . . But the Imam interrupting him called in the guardian of the safe and the guardian said: If Allah wills, the safe is in good shape. And he asked from which budget item it was required that the draft be taken, upon which the Imam wanted to know what were the budget items for which no funds remained, and the guardian replied, All the items except the one reserved for love affairs, adding, Lord Imam, love is something that no one can define for it is not known and yet is known to all. If serious it should be taken lightly, and if taken lightly it can be serious, and God above all is the one who knows.

At these words the Imam called in his Great Writer and asked him what the definition of love was in our cultural heritage, and the Great Writer said that love is that which makes that which does not move, move and stops that which moves from moving. He said that it was not among the things discovered by religion or among the things forbidden in Shariat, adding that it was a cure for every ill, a pleasurable situation, a longed for sickness in which recovery brought no joy and in which consciousness was not longed for. It makes man desire what he previously disdained, changes complex nature, gives and takes in sweet pleasure. Shelter its flames in the heart like a fire in a closed room, strike its flint and it lights up, neglect it and it dies out. If it is not a cornerstone of worship it is at least the essence of all faith.

The Imam threw a quick look of admiration at the Great Writer, feeling dazzled by his vast culture and his knowledge of the cultural patrimony, and just at that moment the Leader of the Official Opposition came in and stood with his head lowered to the ground listening in complete silence, which was a most unusual thing for him, waiting for a chance to reveal the other aspects of this whole question. Until at last almost at the end he managed to intervene by saying that love is harmful vapours rising to the head from congested sperm after a heavy dinner contaminated with nuclear radiation. It is one of the snares of Satan which causes wasting away of the flesh, breathlessness, irregular heartbeats and drags men like us down to a bottomless pit. It is a deadly infection which begins as a game and ends in ruin, and whenever God has sent one of His prophets to this world He has feared for him from the seduction of women, for once a man's organ rises up half of his mind is lost. The erection of the male organ is an overwhelming catastrophe since when it is provoked nothing can stop it, neither the

115

reason of the mind nor faith in God. Love is like war, which rages forwards and backwards, advances to battle and retreats to escape. Women approach love with the faces of angels, and run away with the cunning of devils. They use magic to change a man into a cat or a sheep that crawls on its belly and no man has ever mounted on his woman without her crying out, You have killed me.

At this point the Imam, seized with a great excitement, cried out: Kill her and the sin will be mine. But the Leader of the Opposition said in a quiet voice: Is there enough in the safe for both of us O Lord Imam? What about my share of love? The guard of the safe kept his silence but the Chief of Security quickly asked in his turn: What about me Lord Imam, what about my share of love? There was a gleam in the eyes of the Great Writer as he took them all in at one glance. The guard of the safe broke his silence at last, as though he had decided it was time for him to say something. There is only enough for the Imam and one other man whom he can choose in addition to himself, he said, thinking that the Imam would certainly choose him for as the saying goes, water cannot avoid a thirsty man. The Imam looked around at them as though it was difficult for him to choose between the four pillars of his rule, reluctant to offend any one of them. His life was in the hands of the Chief of Security, his safe in the hands of the guard, democracy in the hands of the Official Leader of the Opposition and the cultural patrimony in the hands of the Great Writer. So the only way the matter could be resolved was by the four of them giving up their share to the Imam, since according to the faith it was he who had the right to all the pleasures of this world and the next, to as many slaves as he liked on earth, and to seventy-seven nymphs at least in Paradise. No one else was allowed the same rights since all men but he are equal before the law and any attempt to change this, to bring in what does not exist, is nothing more than heresy, than falling into a snare prepared by the Devil personally.

So the Chief of Security took the ninety thousand dinars and went round the markets talking to the traders and the brokers, hunting high and low for a slave who would fulfil the wishes of the Imam. He issued orders that no slave

116

quoted at a price of more than ninety thousand dinars should be sold without being shown to him before. But the market was rather slow at the time, for after the defeat in the war most of the slaves and the girls had emigrated to other lands where God had opened up better opportunities for their charms. The Chief of Security went from house to house searching carefully, accompanied by his guards dragging their trained hunting dogs behind them, but he could not find a single virgin who fitted in with the description made to him by the Imam. He was on the point of turning round and going back empty-handed when he caught a glimpse of her running light-footed as a doe with her dog beside her, so he leapt after her, close on her heels, followed by the guards and the hunting dogs panting and straining at their leash. He only had the time to glimpse her from behind as she flew through the night, upright and slender as a spear, her waist like a bracelet holding in the rounded curves where they meet, so that from behind her silhouette had in it all the sacred, inherited and imagined things held in such esteem by the Imam. He lifted his arms up to the sky in gratitude to God. And now there was no longer any chance for her to escape, to slip away from destiny, for the will of God is above all things, and the will of God had decided.

The Imam saw her as she came in. He was lying in bed with his last wife under him, snorting with the effort made in coupling, and without a moment's hesitation he swore a triple oath of divorce, muttering the words through his lips quickly, so that the woman was already repudiated legally before he had time to withdraw. He put on a pair of new trousers hastily and watched her walk in, her back straight as a spear, her head upright in the air, with her dog Marzouk close behind her. The dog looked him in the face just once and recognized him despite the many years which had gone by, for dogs neither forget the heritage of the past nor what happened in history. He jumped on him and caught on to his trousers with his teeth, pulling at them with all his might, repeating what had happened before in history. And since dogs were not permitted to make history repeat itself the Chief of Security caught hold of him around the neck, and

117

quickly put his legs in chains. And that night when all was silent, when all things seemed to sleep, even the wind, he shot him dead with one silent bullet in the head. Meanwhile, the Imam had taken her into his arms, holding her in a close embrace, leaving her with one remaining night in which to live. It was the night of the Big Feast when the moon becomes a full moon once again. She lay on the ground, her naked body bathed in light just as it had been when she was born. She could see her mother's face looking tired and pale and white, and as she lay there on the ground she whispered to herself, I must either save my life or I must die for my sisters. I must deliver them from the tyrant for all time.

Watching through the keyhole of the door the Chief of Security was seized with amazement when he saw her spray the Imam with water from a tin cup, saying all the time, Change your image from the one you have and become a sheep right now, for less than a moment after she had pronounced these words he saw a sheep appear in front of him and the sheep continued to bleat insistently all through the night. But before the sun started to rise she took hold of the tin cup again and spoke a few words into it, then she sprayed the sheep with water and said, Come out of your present image and go back to what you were before, and immediately the Imam became himself once more.

The Chief of Security trembled at what he had seen through the keyhole for it meant that she possessed the secrets of magic and sorcery like her sisters mentioned in the old books. He was seized with wonder at the ability of this slave girl to change the Imam into an animal with four legs whereas he could do nothing to change his own image in any way. He struck one palm against the other in consternation. This could only be the will of God revealing itself through the weakest of His creatures. But he quickly discarded such a possibility and implored God to have mercy on him for his heretical ideas. Such happenings could only be the work of Satan and God was certainly on the side of the Imam and would never allow them to go on. Then a moment later he begged God for His mercy once more, feeling that to put things in that way was also wrong, for God's will was above

118

that of Satan and Satan could do nothing without the will of God. Then closing his lips tightly together as though he had decided never to pronounce himself any more, he screwed his eye to the keyhole and continued to watch what was going on.

The Imam and Bint Allah

It was the night of the Feast and on that night they wed me.
I had no choice. They wrapped me up in a pure white robe
like the clothes of an angel or the shroud surrounding a dead
body and dragged me by a chain tied around my wrist to be
wed. I found myself naked in a bed of rich marble with gilt
decorations like the graves of queens in bygone times, and in
the bed I remembered that I had not seen my mother since
the days of the orphanage when I walked in my sleep,
looking for her. In my dream I hear God's voice calling to
me, and it is like her voice so that I cannot tell between them.
I run towards him and bury my face in his breast, hiding
from devils and evil spirits. I sleep all night and God is with
me and I awake in the morning to Jesus Christ moving his
velvet feel within me. I put my arms around him over my
belly, lift him up to the sun for God, my people and the
Imam to see, and smile in their faces, but they do not smile
back to me. Their eyes go round and round under their lids,
and their faces fall from their heads, and their heads become
red flesh without hair, but their faces are covered with black
hair which is thick, and the soft gentle voice of God becomes
like the howl of a wolf tracking me down in my sleep as I
walk through the night looking for my mother. Behind me I
can hear a loud noise like the noise that the Devil would
make and as I run I can hear the tread of hundreds or
thousands of feet running behind me, like a never-ending
army, and I can feel hundreds or thousands of hands striking
out at me from the back and when I turn round they
disappear, leaving no trace behind them, for they are afraid
to stand their ground and face me. Each one of them is
scared to be alone, and each one of them feels strong only
when he carries an instrument of death over which his hand

is tightly closed. They advance in a straggling line with legs that are bowed and eyes that squint from side to side. I know their faces one by one, the faces of their leaders, and the faces of their dogs straining at their leashes, and each dog wears the face of a lamb by day and the face of a wolf at night, and when they advance the men march in front, followed by the guards, then the dogs, and the cats join in baring their teeth and crawling on small fleshy feet without bones, their eyes shining with lust, their bellies swollen with a foul hunger like stagnant air in closed rooms.

I was running, and as I ran I saw my mother standing near the rock, waiting at the top of the hill which rises between the river and the sea, her arms held out towards me. I almost reached her where she stood, almost reached the safety of her arms away from harm, but I stopped for a short moment when I reached the top to fill my eyes with the beauty of the land, with the peace and calm of the spot where I was born. As I stood in wonder and in love they stabbed me in the back, and before I had time to fall or to forget some letter of the alphabet, I turned round and said: Do you kill the victim and leave the criminal to escape? They said, Who is the criminal whom you mean? And I pointed to the face hanging down from the top of the column reaching to the sky.

And I saw him standing over me as naked as a man could ever be even on the day his mother brought him to the world. I shrank under the covers of the bed like I used to do as a child in the orphanage and said: Who are you? I am the Imam. Do you not know my face? I do not know you, said I. Have you not seen my face before this day? he asked, and I again said, No. How come? said he. Do you not read the newspapers, watch the screens, look at the pictures hanging from the arches of victory, buy postage or excise duty stamps? What are excise duty stamps? I queried. Don't you know what excise duty stamps are used for, girl? he asked. I have never heard anything about them, I said, and he got into a rage and said: You are neither of this world, nor are you one of us, and if you do not know the Imam then you have nothing to do with this land of ours, and if you have no loyalty towards your country, then you have no place for God in your heart. Have you never heard the people when

121

they shout, Long live the Imam, Long live our country, Glory be to God? I said: I have never heard them shout things like that. He struck one palm against the other, greatly surprised. Are you a member of Hizb Allah or of Hizb Al Shaitan? he enquired. Neither, said I. That's very strange, said he. Then are you familiar with our cultural heritage? I do not read, said I. But if you do not read you have at least heard of certain things in it like the Thousand and One Nights and King Shahrayar, said he. Who is Shahrayar? You do not know King Shahrayar who had a wife as fair as honey, yet she betrayed him with his black slave? I do not know him, said I. Then do you know why a white woman should prefer a black slave to her husband although her husband is a king and has a white skin? Because she loves him more than her husband, said I. He struck one palm against the other in great astonishment and said: But can a woman love another man more than her husband? Yes she can, said I. But what can her lover have that her husband does not have? Love, said I. He laughed uproariously with a sound like the beating of drums for the Big Feast and stretched out his arms as though to embrace the universe. My love is so great that it is enough for the whole world, and my heart is so big that it is enough for all my people, he said. If you have a heart which is big enough to include all people then you carry nobody in it, said I.

He rested his head against a gilded cushion stuffed with ostrich feathers, reclining with the weight of his body on a Persian carpet on which was embroidered the picture of the Kaaba, and whenever the glass in his hand shook it spilled over, filling up the depression in the holy stone with some of its amber contents. His naked body was covered in hair but my nakedness was smooth without a single hair except over my pubic area. He fixed his eyes on my body and said: Why do you not kneel at my feet? Throughout my life I have not kneeled to anybody, I said. But I am not anybody, he said, and besides all women kneel. I am not any woman, I said. And pray who may you be? he said. A woman without name, without father, without mother, who can neither read nor write but does not love you and who carries another love in her heart, I said.

The glass in his hand shook so violently that it spilled over completely, drowning the Kaaba, the shrine and the tomb of the Prophet under its contents. The Imam sprang to his feet, standing with them planted apart on the carpet, the hair on his body bristling all over, his bones tense to the very marrow. His lust was now at its utmost, but the vitality of his mind was at its lowest ebb for nothing can inflame his desire and make him lose his reason more than a woman who refuses to be possessed. Now nothing could extinguish the fire which had been aroused in him except one thing, to lay her at his feet and devour her like a vulture eats up the flesh leaving the bones behind.

He sat in front of her sucking her bones, cracking them like sticks of sugar-cane and extracting the marrow from the inside with his tongue and lips. She watched him as she would watch a sheep fattened for the Big Feast enter the butcher's shop, his eyes sinking into their sockets with fear, for in his eyes there was nothing but fear, a terrible fear. No matter how much he ate he was never satisfied and no matter how much he protected himself with all sorts of things he never felt secure. She handed him bone after bone, then gave him the shoulder blade followed by the rump and the spleen. His belly was full up to the brim, swollen like a goat skin, but she continued to hand him one piece after the other until she heard the sound of an explosion and his face fell to the ground. His eyes opened wide with surprise as though he could not believe what was happening and she said to him in a bantering tone, It begins as a game and ends in ruin, then she leapt away light-footed as a doe with her dog running close behind her.

Coming to My Senses after the Ecstasy is Over

In the dark of night my hand groped for her and she took hold of it between her teeth, sharp as the teeth of a cat, and I said to her, You are my little cat, just as I used to call my previous wife Katie who ran away from me and went overseas with her old lover leaving me alone in the other world. I am not your little cat, she said. If you are not a cat, I said, you certainly belong to a breed of tigers. Then she bit so hard on my hand that she cut it off from the arm and as her teeth went through it I felt pleasure with the pain, so I gave her my other hand and again she sunk her teeth into it and cut it off from my arm. This is no game, I said, and gave her my right leg and she held it between her teeth for a moment, then cut it off, and when I opened my eyes as I lay with my face buried in the ground I saw her standing in front of me and recognized her at once, with her thin pale face and the big black eyes, big enough to conceal the crimes of our whole world.

I said to her: You are Bint Allah. Why hide yourself behind another face and inside another body? But she said nothing and stood there completely silent, and I thought, This silence means that she is thinking much more than is permissible in Shariat, for woman was created from a twisted rib and is lacking in both faith and mind. I tried to step up closer to her and make sure that the face I saw in front of me was really that of Bint Allah, but I discovered that I had only one leg and was not standing on the ground, and I started to crawl on my belly towards her while she stood there unmoving and silent. And I said to myself, She is certainly a sorceress and has sprayed me with water from a tin cup while I slept and turned me into a lizard or a sheep, but she

124

did not have the face of a sorceress. In her eyes I noticed a dark glimmer like the eyes of devils and evil spirits so I recited the verse of the Seat several times to chase her away, but she stood there as firm as a rock, her lips sealed in a silence within silence and the silence seemed to vibrate in my ears like the inarticulate turmoil of dying. I stretched out my hand towards her, wanting her to take hold of it, but when I looked at it I saw my whole arm disappear. Then I moved one leg to step closer to her but in its turn it disappeared and soon after my whole body melted into thin air, taking with it all my desires so that nothing was left of me. Then I said to her: Hold my hand in yours, my child, for I am tired of this world and indifferent to all things to the extent where I no longer want anything except to hear you call me father.

My eyes opened wide in amazement and I said: But my mother gave birth to me without a father. No boy or girl is born without a father and I am your father the Imam, he said. I have never seen you before, and I do not know you at all. My father is God and I am Bint Allah, I said. Be silent, and may your tongue be cut out of your mouth, he said angrily. God Almighty was neither begot nor doth he beget children. His voice came from somewhere deep within him as though he was sleeping. He waved an invisible hand in the air and spoke with a voice that could barely be heard. I am tired of the desires of this world, he said, and the only thing I long for now is to open the skull of this woman and crush her brain so that like all the ideal women she will become an invisible body possessing nothing else except a womb. Before his eyes he still had the image of himself which he used to see in the mirror before she had changed him with her magic into a sheep ready to be sacrificed for the Big Feast, and in his ears still echoed the same voice he used to hear delivering his speech, its words mingling with the sound of rockets soaring up into the sky as he stood high up on the platform surrounded by his supporters in Hizb Allah twisting and turning in a belly dance to express their joy, and by the members of Hizb Al Shaitan shouting out their slogans as loudly as they could. He bent his head downwards from the sky to the earth, shifting his look away from the heavens, for

125

he felt that God would support him for all time and that the Devil was also on his side, so why should he fear those whom he knew he could count on not to resist his desires? His eyes were occupied moving from one face to the other, searching all the time, and each one of those standing in the crowd was trying to push his neighbour with his elbows to occupy a place in front closer to the Imam, but his face was turned away from their struggling lines and his look kept sweeping the back rows of the crowd trying to discover a thin pale face and eyes whose colour was like the black of night. Who is he, or who is she, a man or a woman, a human body or a floating spirit? He closed his eyes to sleep but realized he had been asleep all the time with a sleep deeper than that of a tortoise, and nothing could awaken him any more, neither the sound of shots being fired nor the explosions of rockets in the sky.

The Great Writer

I stood in the first row under the bright lights near the Imam. The acclamations of the crowd resounded in my ears and the rockets of the Feast kept bursting in the sky with a crackling noise. Nothing separates me from the throne except the body of the Chief of Security on my right and the body of the Leader of the Official Opposition on my left. I stand between them like an axis held by a rope on either side. If the right rope slackens I lean my head towards the left, and if the left rope tautens I give way with my neck and let my body lean towards the right. I stand holding my back upright, wearing the new suit I bought for the Feast. It is made of the most expensive imported wool and its colour is the dark brown of burnt coffee grains, an indication of my attachment to the right, but I wear a red necktie to show my sympathy with the left. I hold my pen between my fingers by the middle like a stick, keep one foot on the ground midway between Hizb Allah and Hizb Al Shaitan and balance myself on it in a position of stable equilibrium, taking care not to allow it to be shifted from its place.

Even if the earth should tremble with an earthquake I will never shift my foot from its place, for once a man has managed to get a foothold in the front row he should never let go even if the sky collapses over the earth and even if the face of the Imam falls off his head and rolls on the ground, for there are an innumerable number of feet and there is not enough space so that if a foot happens to be shifted, another foot will immediately take its place. Each foot presses up against the heel of the foot in front of it, and each elbow presses into the belly which is beside it like a nail burying itself in wood. But I stand firmly in my place without any movement to one side or the other, balancing my head squarely on my body and keeping my body perpendicular to the ground with my face looking in the direction of the Imam, while the face of the Imam looks in a direction opposite to mine.

He never looks at me, but I am always looking at him, yet at school things were the opposite way round, for he used to sit in class with his eyes fastened on me while I kept my face turned in the other direction all the time. I was top of my class and he came out somewhere at the end of the line, and if I went anywhere he always followed behind. God Almighty, you are the one who alone is able to change all things. You have made it so that he goes before me now, but I swear by Thy name that in my heart I neither rebel nor protest against this calamity, for we must be grateful even for the harm which You do to us, although it is my firm belief O God that You do only good, for it is Satan alone who creates evil. Yet I pray that You will have mercy on me for such blasphemy, for You are the only creator and no one except You can create anything. But why O God reveal the secrets of Your might through the weakest of your creatures? Why give authority to those who are incapable of thinking and deprive those who think of all authority? This indeed is a great calamity and brings with it much evil. But the evil which is brought upon us by God is a test of our belief and we can only accept His will and obey Him. Has not God Himself said: And we shall curse you with evil, for the good of this earth brings temptation? Yet if evil comes from Satan it is our duty to resist it, but how can we tell whether it has come from God or from Satan? Verily I swear O God that I do not stand in the way of Your wisdom, for no one except You, O great changer of things, can make out of good evil and out of evil good.

In the past I had a strong body and a weak spirit, but now I have matured and my body has weakened but my spirit has soared up to the heavens. My legal wife no longer reads what I write and she refuses to respect the Law of Obedience* or the Shariat and keeps arguing with me about things sacred.

---

* A ruling in Muslim jurisprudence which obliges a wife to return to her husband if she has left him without obtaining a divorce.

128

She insists that she has a head on her shoulders and that her head is as good as mine, and this heresy is something the like of which I never heard of with my previous wives whether legal or illegal, permanent or temporary. Not one of them dared to raise her voice higher than mine and if she laughed she would hide her mouth behind her hand and ask God for His mercy. If I beat her according to the rules of chastisement in Shariat she never complained and if I slipped out of bed to go to my mistress she pretended to be asleep and if asleep went into a deeper sleep. But this last wife of mine keeps her eyes wide open and the black of her eyes is so black that it looks darker than the face of the Devil. When she laughs she throws her head back with such abandon that even I am unable to retreat with my head that far, and her laughter is much more spontaneous, much more full of joy than mine, so that it rings out peal after peal as though she is emptying all the air which has accumulated in her belly and her lungs. It makes me feel that inside me are pockets of stagnant air which despite all my efforts to rid myself of them have remained enclosed where they are since childhood. When she laughs her voice provokes more jealousy in me than it does desire, so I leave her lying naked on her bed and rush off to my mistress, who tries in vain to revive my virility, feigning to give herself up to me in complete abandon as though I was killing her under me little by little.

My wife insists that all this is a sign of maturity, a new spiritual strength, the death of the body and the revival of the mind. But I disagree with her completely and say that it is nothing else than a loss of faith in religion and of belief in a moral code; it is all these women who have lost all shame, all sense of decency. And at this she makes a snorting noise and turns on her side, giving me her back and looking up at the ceiling with her eyes tightly closed. I lie there for a few moments, then get up and put on my trousers. When I go back to bed my wife is no longer there, so I lie down alone staring at the ceiling.

On the wall in front of me hangs a picture of my father in a frame. His face looks like mine. It is round and full of flesh, with a ruddy complexion indicating health or a tendency to blush with shyness. He has a straight serious nose like mine, which proves that he is my father and that my mother was faithful to him. His head rises straight up from his body leaning neither to the right nor to the left in the exact stance that my head tends to take. Son, the best line is moderation. Avoid extremes, he used to say, and yet where my mother was concerned he forgot all moderation. She beat him at night and he beat her in the day and yet he would say: Where women are concerned, son, you have to thrash them every day or else expect them to beat you all the way, for we are adorers or adored and there is no middle line to take. But my mother was wont to say: Son, where men are concerned we women are either wives whom they respect but don't desire or mistresses whom they desire but don't respect, and there is no middle way. And as soon as she had said this I could see a grey cloud creep over her face.

She slept with her face to the wall and my father slept with his face to God, while I curled up like an embryo in its womb lying in the space between the two. Every night I listened to my father's voice reading from God's book before he went to sleep, reciting the verse of the Seat three times to chase away devils and evil spirits. When he felt his lids become heavy he pushed the book of God close up to the black pistol he kept under his pillow. His father had given it to him as a present for the Big Feast when he was still a child and whenever he heard a dog bark his hand moved up to the butt of the pistol hidden under the pillow, but if the gland of the Devil started to rise at the lower part of his belly his right hand crept towards it while his left hand found its way under my mother's nightgown to her body. My mother had only to see the gleam of the pistol appear for a moment from under the pillow and she would start to undress with a twisting movement under the bed covers. Yet before she went to bed she would mutter under her breath, asking God for His mercy and protection against the evil and temptations of the Devil. She would do her ablutions five times with water and soap, kneel to God in prayer seven times and wrap her head carefully in a veil, and once she had closed her eyes she fell into the deep sleep of the pious and the pure.

I too slept the deep sleep of a child, seeing nothing and hearing nothing except ghosts and evil spirits. Fear would creep towards me from every side, moving in on me like cold air, so I would keep still in my place in the middle of the bed, moving neither to the right nor to the left, trying not to touch my father or my mother. I feared both of them and with fear hatred stole in under the bed covers with the air, penetrating into my body so that no matter how warmly my mother embraced me I continued to avoid the slightest contact with her, and no matter how much warm affection my father showed me I continued not to love him.

My father was the leader of a religious cult and he used to make amulets for women while they sat with him in the dark of night. It was an occupation which his father had bequeathed him so that through religion he could make the profits he had failed to make by breeding chickens and rabbits. He used to attach the words of God around the women's necks and decorate the amulet with a blue bead hanging from a thread. Then he would return home carrying meat and vegetables from the market but in his pockets he brought back piastres which smelt of the women's sweat.

I would close the door on myself to study my lessons and when the examinations drew close I would remember God, prostrating myself before Him three times with every prayer and imploring Him to help me pass, and God responded to me each time and so year after year I moved up from class to class.

Thus I lived, passing from one success to the other, not knowing the meaning of failure even once. Writer after writer dropped into oblivion but I survived by the side of the Imam untouched. I continued to write without a stop, never reading what I wrote, content to see my picture framed in its box every morning. I spent each day like a short span of life between one dream and the next, and spent each night moving from one level of sleep to the other as I sat with the Imam through the night, drinking toast after toast to our old friendship. Then we stole out together at a late hour to the House of Joy. During festivities and celebrations I stood beside him listening to his speech as he stammered through it with the sun above his head like the open eye of heaven radiating the colours of the rainbow, while all around the crowds shouted out their acclamations, my mind thinking that in this wide world of ours there must be some will more powerful than that of Satan to have made me join Hizb Allah and shout in unison with their voices, Long live the Imam.

As I stand beneath the lights I look around me, searching everywhere for this will which is higher than mine, knowing not where it comes from, knowing only that it lies outside my own being, perhaps falling from the dome of the sky or rising from the depths of the earth, or from the streets and alleys and lanes, or from the tomb-like houses enveloped in smoke, or from the broken looks of those who plough the earth, or from the faces of children covered in flies with their voices twittering like birds, or from the flags flying high on the day of defeat, or from the rockets soaring up in the sky in celebration of the Feast. I stand near the Imam with my foot planted firmly on the ground, for I fear that if I make the slightest movement my place will be lost. I can see the sun like a wide-open eye watching our souls from on high and when the face of the Imam falls to the ground the sky does not change, and the earth does not change, and the acclamations of the crowd go on unchanged, and the rockets still burst with colourful tails, and I still lie near him with my face to the ground as though I have not seen a thing throughout, not seen that the Imam remains the same, that the new Imam is the old one, for even if the body has changed the face is the same, and he still lies on the ground close to where I lie. I can see a transparent cloud float like a mist before my eyes and I can feel dust go up my nose. My head is no longer held well-balanced on my body, and my body is no longer in a straight line with my head, and my foot has been pushed aside and its place taken by another foot, and my eyes peer from under my lids first to the left then to the right, but there is no trace of any of the members of Hizb Allah or Hizb Al Shaitan, nor is there any trace of the body of the Imam.

There I lie alone on the ground and the sun looks down on me with its flaming eye, and the earth under my body is cool, and the voice of my father echoes in my ears like the voice of the Imam, and I look in his direction all the time, but he turns his face away to the other side, and failure runs through my veins and makes my body cry. I close my eyes, preparing for eternal rest, breathing in the dust with slow breaths, dying without haste. Around my neck hangs the key of Paradise but I have plenty of time to savour the joys of the Garden of Eden and my mind occupies itself with the images of the seventy-seven nymphs, some of whom are fair and some of whom are dark, and I am at a loss how to choose from them my heart's desire. The taste of death is in my mouth, a slowly dissolving bitterness flavoured with a sharp tang of pleasure. I drink it down sip by sip like wine bitter at the beginning, sweet at the end. I laugh in a loud voice, letting myself go, at last overcoming my inhibitions, driving the air out of my chest and my belly, my voice ringing out in my ears for the first time more spontaneous than that of my last wife. There is no longer any stagnant air from the days of my childhood held back deep down inside me, nor any feeling of jealousy, nor any desires. I have partaken from the pleasures of this world to the point of satiety and now I have become indifferent, and on my face there remains nothing but an angelic smile.

They took him to his last wife in a tinselled box. His name was printed on the outside in big letters and it carried a large picture of him framed in gold. On his face was a virtuous smile and the picture continued to live in her memory for it had revealed to her the inner sadness in the heart of her late husband. Deep inside her she remembered it as proof of his sensitivity, of his capacity for great sadness, despite the fact that during their life together she had heard him laugh and jest all the time, and although in every encounter as soon as she put her arms around him he slipped through them like a fish. In his absence sadness had brought them together just like love had done before, and year after year went by but she still continued to remember him, and year after year whenever they met she wound her arms around him, but each time like a fish he immediately slipped out of her embrace. She tried to hold on to him, but in vain. Her hands would come out of the sea empty and all that remained behind was his picture in a frame and his words printed in the newspapers, words which neither he nor she nor anybody

133

else except the Imam read. At night she would notice him lying on his back with wide-open eyes staring at his child with an expression of doubt, for the nose was neither his, nor his father's, nor his grandfather's. He caught hold of the little nose with a firm grip as though he was holding in his hand the ultimate proof of her unfaithfulness to him and the child would open his eyes so wide that they seemed to express all the fear in the world, then noticing his father's eyes gleaming in the dark like the Devil, he would shut them as tight as he could. One night he heard his father ask, Whose son is he?, and he heard his mother answer, The son of love. Though still a child he understood that this man was not his father. He closed his eyes happy at this thought and slept peacefully until morning.

Proof of Innocence

He stood upright, his back straight, his head raised to the sky under the sun. On his forehead was the sign of his faith in God, and on his chest was pinned the Star of Victory, and ringing in his ears were the acclamations of the crowd repeated a hundred times, God be with you. His head swayed as the air around him seemed to explode suddenly with a tremendous noise, his face loosened, then folded over and dropped off, falling to his feet as he stood delivering his speech with the Chief of Security on his right and the Leader of the Opposition and the Great Writer on his left. The rockets continued to burst in the sky but his head was no longer lifted high up under the sun and his face had fallen to the ground so that the dust started to fill his nose, but the Chief of Security looked at him as though nothing had happened. He opened his mouth quickly to ask a question before he could forget what he wanted to say: What has happened to the world? The Chief of Security opened his mouth and answered: Nothing, your highness, everything is in order and God is with you. But the body of the Imam shook with anger and he shouted: The hell with me, you idiot, don't you see what's happening?

And the Chief of Security opened his lids wide with an effort and pulled his pupil out of his eyes, looking around with it in the dark until he caught a glimpse of her fleeing through the night as light-footed as a deer. He pressed the muscles of his lips together and blew the alarm and the earth seemed to split open, and suddenly they were all there without exception, members of Hizb Allah or of Hizb Al Shaitan. They seemed to come from everywhere, elbowing their way through, slinging insults at one another, and behind them were their dogs barking all the time. In front was the

Chief of Security running at full tilt with torches in both hands and the others followed, trying to keep up with him from behind. They did not know why they were running, but the order had been given and when the order is given there is no room for questions or discussion, especially as discussion is an invention imported from abroad and has no part in our cultural tradition, and whosoever brings to us what does not already exist in our tradition is plotting chaos and in our religion plotting is a more serious crime than killing. Only a heretic, an unbeliever, a traitor to the nation and the Imam, would dare to argue about such matters, and if it is a woman, then the crime is even worse for then it enters into the realm of vice and dishonour, for honour means defending our land and defending our land means protecting the chastity, the honour, of our women. Nothing is more important than ownership of women's bodies, for men should never have any doubts about the origin of their progeny. The father of every child should be known to all and legitimate children separated from those born of unknown fathers. Since father-hood depends on the father's consent, without this consent a child has no rights and all he can do is pray, fast and repent for his sins, and if the child is a girl her sin is double that of the boy, but she only has half the rights he is permitted to enjoy.

So behind her she could hear the iron-heeled shoes, hoarse voices and panting breaths, the dogs following in their steps. She kept on running without knowing why. The night was dark and in the distant light she glimpsed her mother standing upright, waiting for her there at the top of the rise, calling out in her soft voice, Bint Allah, come here, holding out her arms with an old yearning. Now they were only separated by three steps. She took the first and second steps at a run and there remained only the last one, but she halted at the top of the hill where it starts to slope down again between the river and the sea, stopping to fill her lungs with fresh air and the smells of the place where she came into the world and where she will leave it. She lifted her head up and took a deep breath, filling her lungs with air. The knife went through her back and before she fell or forgot the alphabet she turned around and said: What can be the crime of a virgin never touched by the hand of a man? And they said: When a girl dies a virgin she goes to Paradise but we will not send you to the other world until you are no longer a virgin.

The Chief of Security panted as he wiped his sweat with a handkerchief of the best silk, and the column of men behind him followed suit, wiping their sweat with handkerchiefs of a lesser quality, and the dogs behind the column of men had no handkerchiefs so they wiped their sweat with their paws covered in a dark, cracked skin. The sound of chains rang in the silence like the cries of the crowd on Victory Day, or laughter on a wedding night. Her chained body crawled over the ground like a sheep being led to the butchery. Over the horizon the eye of the sky looked out, burning red, but the angels dressed in white clapped in delight, Hizb Allah beat the tambourines and Hizb Al Shaitan danced to their beat as she lay pegged to the ground, her arms wide open, her legs wide apart with one leg pulled to the extreme left and one leg pulled to the extreme right, the stones hurtling down on the Devil's mark right in the middle of her body. She did not flinch, or move or turn her head. She just lay there with her thin pale face looking up, her wide-open eyes a steady world of unwavering black, her pupil dark as the darkest night in the wider black, her mind clear and bright and crystal white like the moon in the river waters.

In the dark pit dug deep in the earth her eyes remained wide open, always seeing, her memory always remembering a mother's face eternal like the face of God, her ears always hearing the gentle voice calling out, Bint Allah, come here. She raises her eyes to look at the sky and the face of God disappears in the clouds, and the face of Satan looks down at her all covered in hair, the flesh of his scalp bare and red under the sun. She hears the Chief of Security ask: What is your name? My name is Bint Allah, she says. Your name itself is a heresy. Who gave you that name? In the orphanage they called me Bint Allah and I had a sister called Nemat Allah but she died when she was still a child, and I had a brother who died in the war. Did you ever have a sister who died a child, or a brother who died in the war? What is the

137

exact name of your brother? he said, and she answered quietly, Fadl Allah. He nodded his head, wiped his face twice with the handkerchief, prayed God to have mercy on them and said: I know him, I have a picture of him in the file, but his name is not registered either in Hizb Allah or in Hizb Al Shaitan, and this proves he is not one of us, and whosoever is not one of us can only be a creation of the Devil. She said: My brother died a martyr for his country and we fought together in the same trench, and I saw him fighting the enemy with my own eyes. What did you say? he said. You were with him in the same trench? Yes, she said. The two of you alone? That is another crime, for if a man and a woman who have not been married according to Shariat meet alone in a secluded place then Satan will always be there. But he is my brother, she said. He is your foster-brother and your presence together alone is not allowed. In the orphanage we had neither mother nor a foster-mother but we drank milk from the same buffalo. Buffalo or mother it comes to the same thing, he said, for both of them have teats for suckling. He is your foster-brother by decree of the Imam and your punishment is to be stoned until death. I am innocent. I am still a virgin and no one has ever touched me. We will examine you for evidence of your virginity for you cannot be acquitted without material proof, he said.

The Judge

In the dark pit where I lay deep in the earth I saw the face of
the judge emerge into the light. I recognized him immediately
and before he had time to disappear I said to him: You are
the Imam. I am the judge not the Imam, he said. How can
the criminal take on to himself the role of a judge? I asked. I
am the one who is supposed to ask the questions not you, he
said, and immediately after that the last light went out and
the night was so dark that whether I opened my eyes or
closed them it made no difference for the black of the night
stayed black. The cold air seemed like waves of an invisible
sea and his words landed heavily in my ears like drops of
molten gold.

There he stood in front of me wearing a black sash over
his naked flesh, his bald head shining, his face covered in
hair, his eyes sinking deep into the bottom of their sockets.
Do you not recognize my face? he asked. Yes, it is the face of
the Imam, I said. I am not the Imam, I am the judge. Do you
not see that I am the judge? he asked. Since I have never seen
a judge all my life, how can I tell? Have you never seen my
picture in the newspapers? I never buy newspapers, I said.
Why do you not buy the newspapers then? The price of a
newspaper can feed me for three days on bread. But a
civilized person does not live on bread alone, he said. Are
you not interested in culture? Are you a woman or an
animal*? he asked. The price of a buffalo is more than that
of a woman, I said, and a man will have only one buffalo
and yet will marry four wives. And when I was a child in the
orphanage I had no mother so I was nursed by a buffalo, and
I had a sister who died young and a brother who died in the

* Meaning buffalo.

139

war, and did you ever have a sister who died a child, or a brother who died fighting in the war? I said in one breath.

The Imam died fighting and the Prophet died fighting, and Jesus Christ died smitten by his enemies, and I have never stopped fighting the battles that our Prophets fight, he said. In the last session the Imam appointed me to be a judge and ordered me to teach people all that I had learnt from him as a boy. The human spirit lives through four different phases but in not one of these phases does it adore living in heresy and in sin like Namrud and Safrut and Awizra'a* who spread heresy at the time of the Prophet. I saw God in my dreams long before any of the members of Hizb Allah or Hizb Al Shaitan even had a glimpse of Him and I have seen the Prophet on the night of the Revelation† before the Big Feast. In fact I have seen all the Prophets, starting with Adam and Noah, Joseph and Aron, David and Solomon and Zakaria down to Moses and Jesus Christ. I stood in front of the Prophet with my head upright but my soul shrank in humility within me. And as I stood there down came Gabriel, peace be with him, in the form of an angel and carried me far away on his wings so that I could see to the end of the world, further than anyone else has ever seen. I closed my eyes and opened them again only to find myself in the highest kingdom of heaven where stands the tree of thorns‡ overlooking the infinite infinity of the universe. There I heard God call me, saying judge of judges, remove the mist which lies over your eyes so that your sight may be renewed, your face renewed, and your spirit renewed. My memory at once became as clear as crystal so that I realized immediately that I was the very soul of the Imam, that I was none other than the Imam in his previous phases and that God had delivered to me all the secrets of the universe, of the sciences and of medicine, so that I could recognize a sickness and prescribe its cure, tell who speaks the truth from he who lies, know the voice of God from the voice of Satan, a woman with

* Imaginary devils or evil spirits mentioned in incantations.
† The night when the full moon appears at the end of the month of Thoul Higa, indicating the first day of the Big Feast.
‡ The thorn tree from which twigs were taken to make a crown for Christ when he was crucified.

child from a woman whose belly is empty, a virgin girl from a girl who is no longer virgin, the sex of a child before it is born, a legitimate father from an illegitimate one. Now I could also treat women who suffer from menstrual pain, sexual hunger or sexual lust which exceeds the ordained limits, and indeed I do give to every woman a part of my secrets proportionate to the good she giveth to me and to the charity she giveth to others for the sake of God. For those who give generously shall be rewarded and if you give me a part of what good God has bestowed upon you I shall tell you whether you are a virgin or not and whether the child in your womb be it male or female is the fruit of virtue or of sin.

Her face turned white as though all the blood had been suddenly drained from it. I swear that I am a virgin and that no man has ever touched me, she said. If there is a child in my womb it can only be Jesus Christ, for God has visited me in my dreams several times. And he shouted: Silence. May your tongue be cut out of your mouth. Remove your clothes so that I can examine you, for I am the one to know whether anyone has touched you, be it man or spirit, for there are evil spirits that go with women in the dark of night. Take your clothes off, and be not afraid of anything.

She trembled as she took off her clothes and her teeth could be heard chattering. She lay down on the table and on the wall above her was his big hand, a huge black shadow with five fingers. As she lay there two invisible arms stretched out and tied her arms and legs to the four white marble columns of the table and their cold went through the bones of her back as she lay there naked staring at the ceiling above. He stood looking at her in silence, then pulled the curtain over the door and the room was plunged in a darkness deeper than the dark of night. He stood there almost touching her but she could not see him and he continued to stand beside her motionless as she lay listening to the world while the world looked on in silence.

Suddenly she heard two hands creeping over her body where it lay on the table and she tried to pull herself out from under the heavy blanket of the night, but her body was tied down by the ropes. She heard him blow out air once and

141

twice and thrice and each time he blew, her dead body died a little more like the bodies of the dead kept in a morgue, yet each time the flames in his body went higher and higher like dry sticks added to a fire. She lay with her arms open in supplication to God but the flames rose more and more as though he could not stop, like the god of war and destruction burning new victims for his lust. In the dim light she saw a hand emerge from a small cleft in the depths of the earth, first the big finger with no nail, then the small finger with a long nail, then the palm of the hand smooth and hairless, then its back covered with rough dark skin and tortuous blue veins and black spots like old freckles or roots of hairs which had died and dropped off. She heard his voice ask her to blow the air out of her chest and each time she blew she felt her face touch the wall. Slowly she was getting closer to the shadow on the wall, and slowly she moved her face towards it, but inside her she could not find the strength to look at it. She saw it like a tall giant turn round and come back on her where she lay and the invisible hand crept out again and squeezed her nose or the nipple of her breast, she could not tell which, then there was more blowing and a tongue of fire leapt up, stunted at first then growing taller then smaller, then twisting and dancing and burning into her flesh.

She lay in the dark and the wound in her body was a deep gash reaching down to the bone, and under her body was a ribbon of red blood. She could hear the songs being sung for the Feast, the voices of angels rising in a hymn of praise, the ringing of church bells and the crowing of cocks announcing the approach of dawn. Then came the call to prayer, the sacrifice of the victims in the slaughter yards where they were tied, and the acclamations of the crowds multiplied by the microphones a thousand times as they cried, Glory to God, our nation and the Imam. He stood on the platform making his speech. On his right were the members of Hizb Allah and on his left the members of Hizb Al Shaitan, and on the balcony reserved for the harem were the legal wives mounted on their sharp, pointed high heels and surrounded by the women of the charitable societies, the model mothers, the widows of martyrs, the children of God dressed in robes

142

made of white calico, the school children wearing the uniforms of scouts, the girls from the House of Joy in dancing costumes snapping their fingers with the brass discs to the beat of a tune. Up into the sky soared the coloured rockets celebrating the Feast, and below on the ground the beat of drums and tambourines mingled with the wail of pipes, the hallelujas of joy, the screams of pain and the sharp burst of bullets fired from a gun.

But the uproar in her ears is like a silence she cannot hear, and the gash in her flesh is a wound which bleeds without pain. She leaves her body lying there, turns away from it with no regret, and stands up on her feet. She walks on the earth without a body, like a spirit or a dream with feet that do not touch the ground as she moves here and there. Her face is pale and thin with wide-open eyes and thick lashes, the pupils black and seeing. Her mind is like the river water, pure and flowing and crystal clear.

Near the outer door I saw the women. They were dressed in black robes and were standing in long lines waiting for their turn to go before the judge. They struggled with each other, fought with their elbows, each one hoping to get in first, for at the touch of his blessed hand the sick woman is cured, the barren wife becomes pregnant and the pregnant woman empties her womb, the guilty woman is made innocent, the spinster marries, the paralytic rises up and walks, the bedridden woman stands, the healthy woman becomes infirm, the mad woman regains her reason and the reasonable woman is cured of all reason by God, the open eye is closed and the closed eye opens, for he is the judge and by order of the Imam God has revealed all the secrets of the sciences, of law and of medicine to him, and for every measure of secrets which he reveals to a woman there is a measure of good which she must give for what she has received.

I remembered now that I had paid before going in to him. In the dark there was a box hanging down so that each woman could pay without being seen. The voice of the crier went down the lines of women standing at the door, whispering: Pay, O Servants of God, for by the will of God he who gives today shall receive tomorrow not only in Paradise but

143

also in this world from the Bank of Faith* under the patronage of our Lord the Imam. Allah is All Supreme. He is the Abundant who giveth to the rich and all wealth is His but He provides it for our use. Wealth is owned by the God of the two worlds, yet He asketh people for charity and loans. 'He who giveth to God a good loan shall be compensated many times over.' Contribute, O Servants of God, to the fund of the Bank of Faith blessed by God and you will be paid over fifty per cent for we speculate in gold and do not fear bankruptcy. Come forward, O ye men and women of good faith, for with God your interest will reach seventy per cent. Pay in secret and let no one see you, for charity given in secret dispels the wrath of God and cures the sick. The barren women shall bear children and the paralytic shall walk. Fatima the daughter of the Prophet used to imbue the dinars she gave in charity with sweet-smelling perfume and when she was asked why, replied, I heard the prophet say that a dinar given in charity passes through the hands of God before it goes to the poor.

I pull the belt tight around my belly, eat not nor drink, throw piastre after piastre into the hands of God, then close my eyes and fall asleep with the deep sleep of children. In the dark I open my eyes and hear the voice of God calling to me in my mother's voice, warm and soft as her bosom. I run towards it and from a distance I see her standing in the dark waiting for me with her hands stretched out. I have one step to go before I throw myself into her arms but I cease running for just a moment to take my breath and they stab me in the back, why I do not know, and I turn round to face them before I can forget my words or the letters of the alphabet and I say: Why do you strike when I am giving all I have to God? They say: We were speculating in gold and the Bank of Faith went bankrupt because you are a daughter of sin and a bad omen and you brought us bad luck and God will never make us victorious and multiply our profits until you are wiped off the face of this earth.

* Reference to banks which call themselves Islamic Banks and engage in all kinds of speculations, maintaining that they do not pay interest but profit since to pay interest is usually prohibited by Islam.

The Grievance

I asked: To whom can I complain? To whom can I have recourse in my grievance? And they said: The Imam, he is our ruler. Can I complain about him to him? I asked. We all complain about him to him, they said. Complaining to anyone but God is a humiliation*, I said. I folded the grievance I had written and hid it in my bosom so that no one should see it, but the spies of the Imam spotted me, for his spies were everywhere. They asked, What are you hiding in your bosom? Nothing, I said. They opened up my bosom and found the grievance folded up inside written in my handwriting. They held on to it tightly with their hands and said: Now we have the material evidence of your great crime. How can you dare put down on paper and in your own handwriting your grievances against God? I said: It's a grievance against the Imam. Do you not know that the Imam is the representative of God on earth and whoever opposes the Imam, opposes God? I do not know that, said I. How is it you don't know? Don't you read the newspapers? Aren't you living in this world? I do not read your newspapers and I do not live in your world, I said. That is another heresy, a new crime. Whosoever brings us something which we did not have before causes evil and is plotting to create chaos and plotting is much more dangerous a crime than killing.

The judge passed a sentence of death on her and said she had committed three crimes: conspiracy, breach of honour and heresy. Before they executed the sentence and prayed the prayer of the absent over her soul, they asked her in very gentle tones: What do you want before you say farewell to this world? She said: I want a public trial and a proper legal

* A popular saying.

145

defence counsel. They said: We have a legal opposition but we have never heard of a legal defence counsel. They disappeared and came back dragging the Leader of the Official Opposition along with them. He stood in front of her wearing a white turban wrapped around his head, symbol of his devotion to the cause of justice. On his breast he had pinned a red star, the official badge of Hizb Al Shaitan. I am at your disposal, he said in a mellow voice. She looked him in the eyes and said: I am innocent of everything, of crime, of a father, of a mother. . . . But he interrupted her quickly: Of a father? Yes, she said, of a father. He paused a moment, then nodding his head slowly said: This is indeed a calamity and it can only have been sent to you by God for a purpose, for the verse says, 'We have sent you the calamity of evil, for good can be a cause of temptation'. Do you not know this verse? he asked. No, she said, I do not know it. It is a very well-known verse, the thirty-fifth verse of the Sourat* of the Prophets. Have you really not heard it before? he said in a voice expressing profound astonishment. I do not know it, she insisted. Your not knowing this verse is indeed a great sin, he said. You should learn it by heart before the time comes for you to die. It is only thus that you will go to heaven instead of hell.

He put his hand into the pocket of his expensive trousers made of the very best material and extracted a piece of paper and a fountain pen covered with a gold cap. He held the pen between the tips of his fine shapely fingers like those of legal wives and wrote on it in clear black letters: We have sent you the calamity of evil, for good can be a source of temptation. Then he put the gold cap back on the pen, screwed it round three times and returned it to the pocket of his expensive trousers, his fingers reappearing after he had done this as smooth and white as usual. Then speaking again in his mellow voice he said: Repeat this verse three times a day before meals and three times a day after meals and then if God wills you shall find yourself in Paradise.

She held the piece of paper between her finges like a child clutching on to a straw in the stormy seas of life, and

* Literally, picture and meaning chapter.

146

continued to recite the verse day and night until she had learnt it by heart. Through a crack in the door she could see them digging a pit for her in the ground, then they tied her with ropes of hemp and all the time she continued to recite: We have sent you the calamity of evil, for good can be a source of temptation. But the ears of the Imam heard her as she recited, for he had ears everywhere, and he was very angry at what he heard. Do you make mistakes even when you recite the words of God? he said. What mistakes? Is it not a verse of the Koran? I asked. All mistakes can be forgiven except those related to the words of God, he said, for they are more grievous than any other mistake. But what mistake did I make in the verse? Do you not know the correct words? he asked. The correct words are, 'We have sent you the calamity of evil, for good can be a temptation', and you are saying instead, 'We have sent you the calamity of good, for evil can be a temptation', and thus you have made a grievous mistake against God because the calamities which He sends can only be evil and not good. But I did not know what the verse is, I said. Then from where did you get the words of the wrong verse? he asked. From the Leader of the Official Opposition, I said. You are lying. The Leader of the Official Opposition could never make a mistake in the words of God.

The Imam pressed the bell with the tip of his finger and the Leader of the Official Opposition appeared at once with his head wrapped in the white turban and the red star pinned over his breast. Yes my Lord, he said. And the Imam asked him about the verse. But the Leader of the Opposition denied that he had had anything to do with this woman. I only meet virtuous women, he said. And without exception they all believed him, whether they were members of Hizb Allah or members of Hizb Al Shaitan, and they would not believe what this sinful woman had said. So she pulled out the paper that he had written from her bosom and showed it to them, but they said that it was not his handwriting and that now she had committed another crime, which was falsifying the verses of the Koran and forging official documents. I swear that he wrote this paper in front of me with his fountain pen which had a golden cap, I said. What? they asked. What is

147

that you said? A fountain pen with a golden cap? I saw it with my own eyes, I said. Are you accusing the Leader of the Official Opposition with embezzlement? I'm not accusing him of anything but. . . . Do you not know that he was appointed by decree of the Imam and that if you cast a shadow on his reputation you are casting a shadow on the reputation of the Imam? they said. I do not know that but I would like to say . . . But what can you have to say after what you have already said with that tongue of yours which is the source of all rumours and should be cut off from its roots in accordance with Shariat?

At this point her ears had ceased to hear their voices. She stood steadfast in her place without moving, her eyes shining like stars in a black sky and her head raised upright to God. By her side squatted her dog Marzouk, his head lifted up like hers, his ears erect as he strained himself to hear their voices, his eyes vigilant, watching their faces so that later on he would be able to recognize them and when he met the Imam he would bark out as loudly as he could, get a hold on his trousers with his teeth and never let go. They pulled at him with all their might but he continued to hold on tight and refused to let go. They shot him several times from behind and he fell by her side. Between his fangs they found a piece of the Imam's expensive trousers and by its touch you could tell that it was of the very best wool.

The Super-Powers

I raised my head to the sky and lifted my hand to the roaring crowd and that is when I hear the sound of shots being fired. I see my face fall off my bare head and roll under the seat of the throne. I bury it in the ground, hiding it from the eyes of those around, and quickly replace it with the other face which has the features of the Imam. Then I climb back quickly to the elevated platform before anyone has had the time to see me as I fall then rise again. But the world around me now is no longer the same world as it was before. On my chest I can no longer see the medals and decorations I used to have, nor do I see the Star of Justice attached by a pin to my robe, nor is the royal ring on the middle finger of my hand. Not a single one of my supporters remains behind, and the members of Hizb Allah and Hizb Al Shaitan are nowhere to be found. Even my legal wife has disappeared, leaving no trace behind.

I am all alone with no one around and as far as the eye can see the land is a desert of sand. Far away near the horizon I can see a river and behind the river is a green hill. I say to myself, I must have moved to another world and what I see in the distance is Paradise. My mouth has always been dry and ever since I was a child I have always suffered from a great thirst. I am one hundred per cent sure that I will get into Paradise, just as sure as I am of the existence of God. In my pocket I carry a letter of recommendation from the Prophet and several bonds of repentance from the Bank of Faith. I pulled all these papers out of my pockets when I stood in front of the door-keeper Radwan, God's peace be on him. He was illiterate and could not read the words written on the papers. I told him I was the Imam and quickly delivered one of my famous speeches, but not knowing the

Arabic language he did not understand anything and left me standing at the door for a long time with my bare head exposed to the burning sun. I asked him how it was that he did not seem to care much for my speeches, whereas people all over the world were very interested in what I said, and he nodded his head in a way which showed that he had misunderstood.

At that moment I noticed a woman approach from a distance and when I looked at her face I thought that she was my mother but when she came up closer I realized that she was not my mother but my first wife. I begged her to intervene with Radwan on my behalf but she said: The only one who can do anything for you is your new wife. So I said to her: Please help me to find her. Then I saw the town crier advancing to where we stood and I heard him crying out: People of the afterworld, lower your eyes to the ground, the wife of the Imam is passing by. And I saw a fair-skinned woman with the features of a foreigner who looked about the age of my daughter. She resembled my legal wife so I greeted her and said: In the world I wrote many speeches beginning 'In the name of God' and ending with 'Praise be to the Prophet' and so I deserve to enter Paradise. But pointing to the cross hanging over her breast she asked me: Was there no mention of Jesus Christ or of the Virgin Mary in the Koran? So I said to her: I beg of you to intervene on my behalf with them.

She gestured to me to follow her and I held on to the tail of her mare. I noticed that the mare in order to avoid the crowded streets and traffic lights on the earth flew up into the air and that she had a steel wing on either side of her body and a cone-shaped head like the front part of a rocket. I said to my wife, What is this? and she answered, Allah has sent you a new plane as a gift to replace the old mare. So I sat on my seat in the first row with the Chief of Security next to me. Through a crack in the door I glimpsed the face of the pilot. It was round and fleshy and his complexion was very white with black spots on it like freckles and when he spoke he had a foreign accent. When he came to greet us I welcomed him warmly as I always do with the representatives of the Great Powers. He offered me caviar on a silver

plate and a bottle of the best wine and when it was time for
take-off I heard his voice somewhere near the ceiling of the
plane reciting verses of the Koran and praying to God that
He protect the plane from falling to the ground. By God's
grace the plane took off safely and now I could hear the
sound of dance music accompanied by what sounded like the
snapping of a woman's fingers to the beat of the tune. I
looked up and recognized her face immediately. Gawaher?
In those days I was still young and innocent and full of
audacity and Gawaher lived in the House of Joy where I
used to visit her quite often.

As I was thinking of all this the plane shivered suddenly
and we clipped the belts around our waists and once again
the voice near the ceiling started reciting verses from the
Koran and praying to God to protect the plane from falling
as it landed. I felt the wheels of the plane skidding gently
over an expanse of green, soft and smooth like the finest
grass, and I said to myself: We have arrived in Paradise. But
my legal wife said: No not yet, for you cannot enter Paradise
unless Christ pleads for you and until you have paid off the
debts you owed in the world. The man with the black
freckles asked: Haven't you paid your debts yet? Give me
another year, I said, then I can ask God to postpone my
death another year until I have paid my debts. And I gave
him a glass of wine so that we could drink to friendship, but
he refused to take it, saying in his foreign accent that alcohol
is forbidden and that he had been asked to throw all drink
out of the windows of the plane. So I said to him: But
Khawaga,* why prohibit what God has sanctioned? Look
at God's Paradise and you will see rivers flowing with wine
and beautiful nymphs as fair as honey. He looked over the
fence but could not see anything. Where is the Paradise you
are talking about Lord Imam? he asked. Wait, I said, patience
is a good thing and no one should try to hurry God. By His
will we shall enter Paradise together. You go alone and I'll
wait for you in the plane, he said. Take-off time will be
exactly six o'clock GMT and remember I'll be waiting for
you just in case, God forbid, anything should happen to you.

* Foreigner, a slightly derogatory term.

151

My legal wife took my arm and we went off to meet Christ. She whispered in his ear in a language I did not understand. He nodded his head and said that he agreed to mediate on my behalf, then enjoined us to follow the straight and narrow path of God, but when I put my foot on it I could not advance even an inch. My legal wife looked at me and said: This is where I shall have to leave you to the good hands of Allah and His Prophet. And she went off leaving me trembling all over, but I noticed a black woman running over the straight and narrow path as fast as she could and she caught hold of me by the hand before I fell off. I recognized her face immediately, for she had been my slave before God opened the doors of good fortune to me. I had run away from her in the night just before she gave birth to my daughter.

You are the first and only love of my life, I said. And I walked along beside her leaning to the left whenever she tried to hold me up on the right and bending towards the right whenever she tried to hold me up on the left until we were both exhausted by the effort. So I said to her: Gawaher, if you want to help, then the best thing is to do according to the common saying, 'Mistress if you are at your wits' end what to do, carry me Za'afouna'. Now what does Za'afouna mean? she asked. It means hang your hands over the shoulders of the other and grasp hold of both his hands, then lift his body up with his back facing your belly. Have you not heard what the Gahglouls* of this world have said: 'My situation has advanced so much backwards that I now walk backwards Za'afouna'? I have heard neither of Za'afouna nor of Gahglouls, she said, but whatever they may be I shall still carry you to the Prophet Mohamed. And when we got to the Prophet Mohamed, peace be on him, he said: I bestow this black woman on thee. Take her with thee so that she might wait on you in Paradise. But no sooner had we arrived at the door of Paradise than Radwan looked at me severely and said: Have you got a pass? And I said, No. There is no way of getting into Paradise without a pass, he said.

I stood there waiting for a long time under the hot sun

* Names given in folkloric stories to those who are failures or slothful.

until my bare head felt like an oven and it was almost time for the plane to leave, when I noticed that near the door there was a willow tree. I asked him to give me one of its leaves so that I could go quickly back to the Prophet and get a pass on it, but he said, I cannot let anything out of Paradise except with the permission of His High Majesty. If he sees me He will know me at once, I said, for in the world we were together all the time. I had many supporters in Hizb Allah and innumerable friends inside the country and abroad, and many of them were kings and presidents and great leaders, and when I died they all walked in my funeral. It was really an awe-inspiring thing to see. Did you not see the picture in *Newsweek*? Never heard of *Newsweek*, said Radwan. If you have never heard of *Newsweek*, I said, then you certainly know neither the great men of the world, nor the Great Powers.

The Mother's Vigil

The noises echoed like a deep silence as I stood with my bare head under the scorching sun. In my chest I felt a sharp pain like a wound or a hole penetrating through to my heart. The door of the other world was still closed, while the first, second, third and fourth worlds continued very much as usual without me, and the man standing on the platform to receive the acclamations of the crowd was not me but someone else. The rockets of the Feast were still soaring up into the sky and the door-keeper of Paradise was still examining my passport, his eyes peering at my photograph from under his dark glasses as he asked me one question after another. I explained to him that I was carrying a recommendation from the Prophet and that I wanted to see Allah. He asked me whether I had an appointment and I said no but if He saw me He would receive me at once. He enquired whether the object of meeting God was something official or private. Official, I said. What is the official question which brings you here? At this I lapsed into silence, not knowing what to answer. Official things are not considered a secret, he muttered after some time, looking askance at me from under his dark glasses, reminding me of the Chief of Security when he used to interfere in things which did not concern him.

Once more he left me standing at the door for a long time and taking off the telephone receiver plunged into a long whispering conversation with some woman at the other end of the line, every now and then bursting into loud laughter but careful always to address her using masculine pronouns. I kept my silence, not wanting to spoil his mood. When he had finished he noticed that I continued to stand there and said: You're still here? I implore you, let me meet Him, I said. Why do you insist on meeting Him? he repeated again.

154

I want to ask Him to postpone my death for a year, I said. A whole year, he exclaimed. Really you exaggerate, say a month or a couple of months at most. Master Radwan, I said, one month is not enough to re-arm the army, pay back our debts and restore the morale of our people after the defeat. I do not want a year because I'm still interested in the pleasures of life or the frills of the world. I want it in order to serve God and the cause of the nation.

Just then the telephone rang and he started a converstion with another woman, but his tone this time was sharp and peremptory and he ended it quickly, so I realized she was his legal wife. Before the telephone had time to ring again I said: I am still awaiting your instructions Master Radwan. By this time he had become absorbed in the papers on his desk. He lifted his eyes from them and looked at me from under his dark glasses for a long moment, then said: Drop in tomorrow. But my previous experience with security guards now came to my rescue. I took something out of my pocket and handing it over to him said: Take this double gift to your Master and ask Him to meet me today for I have no time and my plane is waiting for me. He pocketed the gift, looked at his watch and said: You only have a few minutes to catch your plane, and so it's better for you if you leave immediately, but I will send you a notification by post if you leave me your address. I gave a look of doubt in his direction but then retreated, remembering that he was our Master Radwan and could not possibly be lying. Since he had promised, he would certainly do what he had said. So I left him my address and went off to the airport, but deep within me was the certitude that he was never going to send me a thing.

At this point I had reached the limits of despair and I slackened my pace, seized with the feeling that I no longer cared if I missed my plane. I sat down overcome by exhaustion and no sooner had I laid my head on the ground than I fell asleep. As a result I neither heard the sound of the plane when it landed nor did I hear it when it took off. I woke up with the firm conviction that I should expect nothing since Radwan would certainly not send me the letter despite his promises, and even if I saw him coming towards me with a letter in his hand I should not expect it to be for me. In fact

155

even if it turned out to be for me I should consider it a mere accident in which something had gone wrong in God's calculations, so that if Radwan did come to me with the letter, then rather than holding out my hand to take it I should tell him to continue on his way since the letter was certainly not meant for me but for someone else. I could no longer see God addressing a letter to me since I knew I did not deserve it, and at this thought I smiled with a calm contentment, indifferent now to everything, even to the idea of meeting God. I said to myself: God, all I really want is a rightful compensation, neither more nor less, since I was the one who had the courage to proclaim a firm intention to apply the laws of Shariat and to do everything in my power to ensure that Your precepts are executed in their entirety, including enforcement of the maximum punishment for adultery and theft, and throwing all alcoholic drinks into the waters of the river. No one of those who try to ingratiate themselves with You, who whisper soft words in Your ear and throw meaningful glances in Your direction, has been bold enough to take the stand I took, not one of them has stood up for You as I did, or has applied Your Shariat the way I did.

I put my face between my hands and tears started from my eyes at these thoughts, so that I did not hear the voice which spoke in loud imperious tones coming from behind me and which said: Stand up and raise your arms above your head. I refrained from turning round for I realized that no one would speak to me in such commanding tones unless his rank was higher than mine. I stood up at once, raising my hands above my head, expecting the blow to come from behind at any moment, but instead the voice ordered me to turn around. I found it difficult to believe that anyone seeing his enemy from the back would give him the chance to turn around and face him since assassination from the back is certainly easier than it is if done from in front. This order to turn around could only signify contempt and if contempt for an ordinary man is the worst insult, then how should it be met if the object of contempt is the Imam in person? I stood my ground, refusing to turn around and face the voice. It was better to end up an assassinated Imam rather than to become an Imam of diminished stature, so I kept my feet planted firmly on the ground with my arms lifted high in the air above my head, then I threw myself headlong to the ground with a valiant smile on my face like a warrior caring little about life or its worldly desires, ready to meet death at any moment.

The rustle of tree leaves and the croaking of frogs were like joyful music in my ears and the night breeze was cool and refreshing, carrying with it the smell of the sea. There I lay steadfast as a rock, unbending, refusing to move, or to run, or to pant. I had plenty of time for there was no longer anything important or unimportant in my life, anything I was afraid of missing. I no longer felt pain or despair, no longer cared, no longer thought of Hizb Allah or Hizb Al Shaitan, no longer saw images go through my head except that of myself as a child nursing at my mother's breast with the warm milk running gently down my mouth. Suddenly I choked, then gasped, opening my mouth wide and closing it several times like a fish out of water, beating the air with my arms and legs. My face was turning blue as I choked more and more, as though at any moment I would suffocate and die, leaving the world without an Imam, without a representative of God on earth to deal with the affairs of our world. But my mother gave me a hard slap on the back, expelling the milk from my air passages or expelling the air from my milk passages, making the blood flow back to my face and awareness flow back to my mind so that I noticed her face in front of me, and suddenly my memory returns and I remember not seeing her at all in twenty years.

I rise to my feet, press my hand over the wound to stop it from bleeding and walk along the old pathway which I know so well and can never mistake. I knock on the old dark wooden door of her house and it opens with the creaking noise of a water-wheel. I can hear the sole of her foot tread over the floor as she moves up behind the door and her voice which I can never mistake for another voice comes to my ears from afar. Who is it? It's me, I say, and I can hear her heart beat, her breathing hard and her rough hand shake as she opens the door. Her tears are a white mist over the eyes, her lids without lashes, her back old and bowed. Twenty years have gone. Then she had lashes which were dense and

157

black and long, and a back as straight as a spear. She put her arms around me and her tears wet the expensive wool of my official suit. Twenty years my son, twenty years since I last saw you, she said. I've had so much to do mother, so many problems to deal with and all of them so difficult to solve that God alone, praise be to Him, can find a solution. Your face looks so pale, she said, that it is as though you haven't had a decent meal in twenty years.

She went to the kitchen, moving with the brisk pace and the straight back of bygone days, her feet flying over the stone floor as though her body had grown light once more. She came back through the kitchen door, her eyes brimming over with happiness, looking at me through dark thick lashes as she carried a tray of pastry and honey and fresh morning milk in her hands. She came up to me where I sat on the old divan near the window, just as I used to sit when a child watching the stars and seeing God up in the clouds looking down on me with a face like my father. I could hear the beat of her heart, see the shine in her eyes, feel the trembling of her hands under the tray shake the plates. She had only three steps to go and her heart went round and round with happiness, and the world was a merry-go-round on which she rode and now there was only one step to go and I could see her trying to make the step, trying to move her leg, but it would not move. She stood in front of me not more than an arm's length away and I saw her drop to the floor. I stretched out my hand to hold her up but it would not move. I held out my arms to try and embrace her but the distance between us seemed to have grown as though we were moving all the time in opposite directions.

The Latest Wife Meets the Illegitimate Daughter

I was not in a hurry to see him sent off in the box. True he was dead but his being there gave me the chance to have some kind of a dialogue with him. When he was alive there was never any dialogue between us, although he wrote article after article about communication through dialogue. He would be silent all the time or talking all the time, with nothing between. He heard only himself and saw only himself and always as a picture either in the newspaper framed in a box or on a tomb of marble. The pen was held always in his right hand and his head was held always with his left hand, as though his brain had to be protected carefully, and yet the writing would not come either with or without pain, like a monthly indisposition which refuses to flow as it should. In the summer he sat drinking wine and swallowing peppered beans, and in winter he stretched himself out in the sun, emitting one yawn after the other until he had rid himself of the fumes around him mind and recovered consciousness. He sat at his desk in the top storey of the biggest building in town, shuffling through the papers in front of him and examining the photographs taken of the Imam and he sitting there close to him at top-level meetings, or in special sessions of the Advisory Council and Parliament, or during celebrations and festivities or at contests for choosing beauty queens or model female martyrs, or at seasonal fashion shows, or during the distribution of prizes to the members of Hizb Allah or Hizb Al Shaitan on Literature and Arts Day. Or he stood in the first row at public meetings, under the admiring glances showered on him from the balcony of the harem by the respected wives of state personalities, widows of martyrs, model mothers and women presidents of charitable societies,

159

all gathered for the occasion around the wife of the Imam. Her smooth-skinned hand blazing with diamonds in the sunlight proffers itself to him, holding the Prize of Finest Literature and a Certificate of Good Morals and Manners by the tips of her fingers, while the small plump hands around her applaud delicately, fluttering like a volley of pigeons, and the square bodies dressed in mourning black balance themselves on the tips of high-heeled shoes and the hearts beating under the ribs seem to repeat, God, the nation, the Imam.

The telephone on his desk never stopped ringing. When it rings he gives me his back, lifts the receiver and whispers into the wires for hour after hour. After he has hung up he says: It is not permitted for a legal wife to surprise her husband in his office like the Chief of Security does. I laugh loudly and say: It was not my intention to surprise you but it is not permitted that a legal wife refrain from passing on her legal husband while on her way to meet her lover. He turns round in the swivel chair to face me with his whole body and when he lifts up his eyes to look at me I can see them shining with lust. He desires me more, the more I desire someone else and I can feel his eyes fastened on me, but I look the other way. At night he tries in vain to possess me, so he takes hold of his pen and tries to write, but fails to write anything and in the morning when he opens the newspaper he finds the same article published for the hundredth or the thousandth time. His face framed in the box is his old face, as old as Adam, peace be on him. Failure invades him through every pore like sweat going in the wrong direction and I can see him struggling against it like a fly in a plate of honey. He wipes his face with a handkerchief and gives me a smile as though overwhelmed by a feeling of sadness. Then he says: I am attainted by writing like a man attainted by disease and writing kills just like love. But I reply: Writing does not kill. Nothing kills but the lack of a real consciousness, and it is not love that kills but its absence.

I can see him look at me with eyes full of jealousy. Deep inside he hopes his consciousness will return to him so that he can write, and deep inside he wishes that he could love like I do so that life would return to him after it had left him behind. The smile on his face remains fixed and I realize that

160

he has hidden his sadness in the heart until death. I used to hear him laughing loudly all the time and thought him incapable of sadness, and I leave him alone in his room to write, but he does not write, and in the morning I see his article filling a whole page of the newspaper with at the top his picture framed in a box, and I look at it thinking it is his new face but I realize it is the old one and that there has been no change.

I lifted my head and saw her face pale and thin with black eyes like two stars shining in the night. Who are you? I said. I am his daughter, she said. But I am his legal wife and he had no daughter, I said. He ran away from my mother and refused to recognize me as his child. You are his illegitimate daughter then, I said. Yes, she said, and when she had said it my eyes retreated before her eyes so far that they hit against my body, shaking it deeply so that my brain was shaken with it and my heart and consciousness came back, making me realize that he was a body in a box and that she was a young virgin and that she and I were the same in many ways for she stood on two legs not on four and so did I, and she had two arms and two hands and each hand had five fingers and she held her hand out to me and bared her breast before me without fear. So I held my hand out to her and our hands met over his body lying in the box and when they met my heart shivered, and she held my hand in her hand with a firm grasp, and I held her hand in my hand and it was the small hand of a child the size of my palm and it was warm, as warm as my body and as warm as my heart. Then our four arms moved towards each other, following our hands in an embrace, and the embrace was close so that our bodies followed our arms and body touched body leaving no space. I said: Where have you been and when were you born and are you still alive? She remained silent, answering nothing, just looking at me with eyes big enough to contain all the sadness of the world. Then walking slowly over to the window she looked out over the universe, opening her arms as though calling out to God or to a mother or a father. Her look fastened itself on the picture set in a frame carved on the box, then swung upwards to the sky over the arches of victory, the domes of churches and the minarets of mosques, and down again to the earth, the streets, the houses, the shops with people drinking glasses of cane juice, children wearing their new clothes for the feast and flying coloured balloons which rose up in the air to the sky, floating under the sun accompanied by the cries of the children, moving with the cool breeze of the river until it met with the cool breeze of the sea. And the voices of the children ran through her body like peals of laughter and she stretched out her arms to embrace their voices, to embrace the sun as though she was the mother.

I stood watching her as she looked out of the window. I heard her breath in gasps, like someone stifling her sobs or gasping with laughter, and her panting gasps went on as though she had been running for a long time and could not stop. I could hear her heart beating with an audible sound and she held her hand over the wound cutting deep into her flesh below the left breast. Her face was white, almost bloodless, her eyes dry without a tear, her pupils black, shining like seeing holes in the sky at night. I heard her say in a whispering voice like the rustle of leaves: I did not cry out when I felt the knife go through my back. I turn around, trying to see where it came from. After a while I stand up again, pressing my hand over the wound to stop the bleeding, then walk holding my shoulders upright, looking at the sun above me. I go through the streets, between row upon row of closed windows and closed doors, and stop in front of the only door which is open. Written on the outside are the words, House of Joy. I said to myself: This is the door which leads to God. I asked about my mother, for I had not seen her since the day I was born, and they told me that God had taken her away. So I thought, if I find God then I will find my mother, and I started to walk in my sleep with my arms stretched out in front of me looking for her in the dark of night. I had never seen God face to face except in dreams, and in the orphanage they used to call me Bint Allah, and when I looked over the high wall I could see the dome of the church and the light of the minaret high up at the top of the mosque. The guardian of the mosque told me that God had neither sons nor daughters, and the guardian of the dome

162

told me that God was the Father, the Son and the Holy Ghost, and that no one had ever heard of Bint Allah.

I had never seen my father and I thought he was God, but later on I heard he was a Great Writer in the court of the Imam, that he had children, money, a good reputation and no enemies whether in Hizb Allah or in Hizb Al Shaitan, and that everybody liked him whether friends or enemies because he led a simple and ascetic life much like that of Christ, except that he shared it with his latest wife whom he never touched except on Thursday nights, after which he went to prayer on Friday mornings without doing his ablutions, kneeling behind the Imam with great piety and devotion. After prayer, still in a kneeling position, he nodded his head to the right, expressing his loyalty and obedience to Hizb Allah, then nodded his head to the left in greeting to Hizb Al Shaitan, and prayed for God's mercy three times before prostrating himself, and after repeating the same prayer another three times he got up to his feet light as a newborn babe, purified of all sin. He would leave the house of worship walking behind the Imam with slow steps and with bowed head, all the time murmuring verses of the Koran on his lips and repeating the ninety-nine holy names of God on the beads of his rosary, and preceded by the Imam he would walk down the narrow corridor leading like the straight and narrow path of God to the wine room on the first floor of the palace. There they would drink glass after glass to their old friendship, recalling memories of their youth when they used to visit the House of Joy together.

Illicit Love

There was a green garden surrounding the wine room of the palace and surrounding the garden was a high wall made of iron bars. In the garden was a wolf dog of the best breed imported from overseas, and at night he had such a fearsome bark that no one would come near the place except brigands, or devils, or evil spirits. During the day they disappeared in tombs or in tomb-like houses and at night they came out, and the Imam would sit under the smooth red lights with a glass of wine in his hand. By his side on the sofa, separated by no more than an arm's length, sat his life-long friend, and filling the space between them was a cushion stuffed with ostrich feathers which hid under it the Holy Book of God written with gold letters and a revolver of the best type fitted with an efficient silencer. Whenever the dog barked the hand of the Imam would creep by itself to feel the butt of the revolver, and the heart of the Great Writer would beat furiously under his ribs, for his smooth fingers had never known the feel of anything apart from his pen. Ever since he was a child he had been afraid of the dark and he had not known what it meant to have enemies. His friends in Hizb Allah and Hizb Al Shaitan were numerous and he gave abundantly of what God had given to him. He nourished friendship with money and people called him the Generous Writer, but his wife said he was a miser at home.

The night of the Feast he came home with empty hands instead of bringing her a gift, and in the morning he would forget to leave her money for the house before he left. He returned home late at night with empty pockets and a lost consciousness, his breath smelling of wine and women's sweat. The lips of his legal wives remained tightly closed and not one of them dared to open her mouth, for if she did she risked hearing him swear an oath of divorce, pronouncing it three times as he lay on his back with his mouth half-open and his eyes half-closed, and after that she would be seen carrying her bundle as she left the house, and the next wife would arrive carrying the fear of divorce in her heart like a fear of death. People always knew all about her husband but she remained always the last to know. She would hear rumours and refuse to believe them, chase all illusions out of her life or hide them deep inside, fearing to reveal them to herself and transfer them into truths she could not deny. Her lips remained closed all the time and she never opened her mouth, and yet the oath descended upon her like fate and along came the next wife with a fear in her heart, as deep as her fear of God. She would never say a word, never allow herself to have the slightest illusion, but divorce would knock at her door for no reason and so would come the turn of the fourth wife as allowed by Shariat. She is young, holds her head high. Her body is slender and lithe and she lies in wait for her fate like a lioness, her eyes wide open and black like a devil. She has read books, read the history of kings and knows the cultural heritage including *The Thousand and One Nights* and the sacred writings. She knows both God and the Devil, Paradise and Hell, does not fear death and is in no haste to see Paradise, for in Paradise there is no place for women who are not virgins.

He went to ask for her hand, carrying the marriage contract in his hand and wearing his virgin's face. He showed her his picture, an enlargement set in a frame, hid his thrift behind generosity, his fear behind love, but he was like his father bedding with another woman and forgetting his mother until it was time for him to die. His mother had nurtured another love than that of cooking and having a spouse. She hid sheets of paper under her bed, wrote stories and collected them one by one into a book. It was her first book and her last, for after she married her fingers never touched a pen. At night after his father went to sleep she would open the bottom drawer in the desk, feel the cover with the tips of her fingers and the letters of her name printed on the book, as though she was holding a precious jewel. She would look around her, fearful lest someone should see her, to find her eyes looking into the eyes of her baby son, wide open in the night like the eye of God watching what she was doing. So she put the book back in the drawer and closed it with a lock, then lay down again on the far side of the bed near the wall, with her husband on the other edge and the child lying on his back between them, his eyes closed pretending to sleep, and in the morning his father would beat him because he had not learnt the lessons of the previous day. Like his mother he hid his love for writing about the things which he felt and continued to study science as though science and art were locked in struggle, learning the words of God by heart, engraving them in his memory, gaining the love of his father and losing his art. In the dark of the night he could feel his father's ear listening intently to the beats of his heart, trying to detect any beat, any drop of art, that might have leaked into him with his mother's milk.

The Mistress

She had come from the House of Joy to take a last look at him as he lay in the box smiling from ear to ear. When he saw her bend over him, he looked up and in his eyes she saw a glimmer of love. A last desperate fantasy which will lead to nothing, she said to herself. His love for women has always been like the struggles he fought in vain against defeat. His legal wives were standing there when she walked in, holding herself upright, her abundant hair wound tight around her head and held up with a white kerchief adorned with black sequins which hung in a row at the edges. Her look moved away from him to the legal wives standing in line, their ample bodies clothed in mourning black, their plump hands clasped over their hearts, their feet shod in high-heeled shoes, their legs pressed together, their breath held in awe and respect for the dead. They looked alike except for a badge on their shoulders or a brooch on their breasts, for their features seemed to have been rubbed away, their heads small like birds on a tree, their haunches prominently displayed, bodies all flesh without spirit, thin lips pressed together in silence, eyes bulging like frogs in a stream or fish in the sea. And suddenly their mouths opened to ask: Who are you? She lifted her head with the pride unknown by a legal wife and said: I am his mistress Gawaher. Their bodies swayed on their high heels, stirring the consciousness which lay buried somewhere, for in her black eyes they saw the pain-giving gleam which spells truth, felt it go through straight to the heart. They asked in one breath: Whose mistress? All of them, she said, starting from the Imam down to the guardian of the mosque's minaret.

Their eyes opened wide in fear and they hid their fear behind their hands, folding their arms around their breasts,

167

closing up like a mollusc closes its shell, and gasping out in one breath: You are the devil and your punishment is death. After that they fled, their high heels rapping on the floors like the sound of rockets bursting overhead. Only two women remained after they went: the illegitimate daughter and the legal wife. They stood with their hands clasped together and after a moment the mistress held out her hands to them and the three women embraced, with six arms holding each other tightly above the dead body lying in the box. The smile on his face vanished and his features seemed to evaporate, leaving a face which no longer resembled that of the Imam or the Great Writer or the Chief of Security or the Leader of the Official Opposition, or anyone in Hizb Allah or Hizb Al Shaitan. His face became faceless, or became the face of all of them merged into a single face without features, so that it was no longer possible to distinguish between one and the other except by a badge on the chest or a star on the shoulder, or something or other on the head.

In the mirrors of the universe was reflected the image of three women with upright heads, their big black eyes staring out like holes in the night and the world looking on in silence.

Gawaher

His eyes looked out at her from the box where he lay with a look full of love. Her hand caressed his head from the top to the nape of his neck, then moved round like a silk thread tightening itself around his neck until he started to gasp for breath. The more she pulled at the thread the more he laughed, and she kept tightening the noose until his face went blue, so she loosened the grasp of her fingers and started to move her hand slowly over his chest, playing with the blue bead which he had worn since his mother had hung it around his neck and which he had never thought of removing. Her fingers started to play with it, to catch hold of it and let it go, like the slender jaws of a forceps. Your mother was afraid for you from the evil eye and I fear for you from the evil ear, she said, pulling at his ear, laughing from the bottom of her heart and throwing her thick hair behind her back with a quick movement of the head.

His ear stood up, straining itself to catch the words of love, and her eyes gazed steadily into his eyes until the roots of the hair on his head became erect, and he hid the white hairs with a dye of black henna sent to him by his mother in a small sack made of calico. He dissolved the powder in water and dyed the hairs once and twice and thrice until they became as black as a moonless night, but the grey hairs on his belly and his chest revealed his age and he kept touching the wrinkles on his face, opening his eyes wide with astonishment, for it was as though old age had crept up on him while he slept. Her eyes met his in the mirror and she looked away at once, fearful as though he had a disease which could infect her if their eyes embraced. In her eyes he could read an expression of sadness for herself, for she was still young and living and he was old and dying. He put his arms around her and wept between her breasts saying, I am defeated Gawaher, and she pushed him away from her with a quick movement of her hand for deep down inside her she knows that he wants to infect her with his impotence. With each encounter between them his failure grows more evident, yet he never ceases to come back to her like someone suffering from an addiction with which he cannot cope, like wine to an alcoholic which breeds a thirst so great that he can neither live nor die without it.

He would never admit defeat to her, for like an addict his exhilaration increased with every moment, giving him a false sense of being victorious. Whenever he was with her he would watch her body as it moved under her clothes. In her eyes was a gleam that showed like the edge of a sword and injected new life into him like a steel needle. His body quivered in her arms like a chicken being slaughtered, but her body was never moved at all. You are different to other women, he would often say. You are a woman who is unconscious of her body and conscious of her mind at every moment. After that he would yawn as though sleep had pounced on him all of a sudden and peer at her with eyes full of jealousy, for he was more jealous of her mind than he was of anything else, sometimes trying to take her by force, to rape her, as though through rape he could restore the balance that was lost between them, only to reveal his impotence more and more. Once he left her he hurried to one of his legal wives to bury his head between her breasts and sob like a child. His wife, still fast asleep, would take him into her arms and his hot breathing on her neck would give her a vague feeling that he was mortally in love with another woman whom he did not know how to possess. Thus in the midst of her sleep she would discover that a woman who belongs to nobody is adored by all men without exception, since she is the only woman capable of inflicting pain on them, and still asleep, she would say to herself: Men love only those who make them suffer.

The Mother and the Daughter

She saw herself standing in the mirror tall and slender. Around her head was a halo the colour of night and her eyes were as large and as round as the disc of the sun. The curves of her body burned with the colours of the rainbow lying over the green hill between the river and the sea. She opens her arms to embrace the world and moves her legs over the earth, her feet treading to the rhythm of music. The melodies of the morning like the harmony of the night move through her body, for she has a mind that knows no rest and a body that never ceases dancing, and the air around is the music which she loves and the music in her breast is the air which fills her lungs. She flies through space like a spirit without body, whirling round and round in a dance without the roundness of a thigh or the curve of a belly, and she raises her head to the sky and captures it but she herself is captive to no one.

In her ear she hears a knock followed by a knock followed by a knock, three knocks that she knows too well ever to forget or to confuse them with anything else. The small face looks out from the clouds and she knows it too well ever to mistake it for anyone else, for she can pick it out at once from among a million other faces. The small hand protrudes from its sleeve, pale white, without a drop of blood under its skin. The eye is big and black like a hole in the night. She hides the small body close to her breast and starts running on and on without stopping and behind her she can hear them treading with their iron heels, for on the bottom of every shoe is a hoof made of steel and in the grasp of every hand is a stone or an instrument used in killing. She lies hidden in her mother's breast close to her mother's heart and her heart beats with every beat of her mother's pulse and her

171

five fingers clutch her mother's thumb, and her mother runs on and on under cover of night before the light of the rising sun breaks out, and the sun lingers to give the mother a chance and the moon too has hidden itself away in some place, and the stars have gone to sleep somewhere else, and so in the whole wide world you cannot find the faintest light even if you search high and low. The guardian has locked the last door in the palace, reciting the verse of the Seat as he slams the bolt, and the Imam is fast asleep and so are all the members of Hizb Allah and Hizb Al Shaitan, and even the wind and the trees have gone to sleep.

She stands and looks around, fearing to be seen. Then having made sure that all is clear she wrenches her away from her breast and starts to make a smooth bed with the palm of her hand, brushing the pebbles and stones to one side and sprinkling soft earth over the surface of the ground to make it like the bosom of a mother, and when everything is ready she lays her gently down. Her face is a pale patch looking out of the wrappings and her teeth chatter with cold, so she removes her black woollen shawl from her shoulders and wraps it closely round the small body. Her small hand touches the finger of the mother and the five fingers curl around it closely, taking a tight hold. The mother lets her hold on to it for a long moment, for as long as the sigh which goes through her, for she had forgotten that they were after her and that the distance between them had shortened. She let her finger lie in the little hand until her very last breath, until she stood up looking down at her and they stabbed her in the back, one stab after another without stopping, so she turned her face away from the child, refusing to look at them, and they continued to stab her from the back right through her body. But her body continued to stand up, refusing to bend or to fall from its upright position, for it had already fallen before, and when something which has fallen falls it can only rise up once more.

They shouted at her as loud as they could but she continued to give them her back for she knew that as soon as she turned round to face them they would run away. They could not bear her eyes on their faces, knowing full well that she knew them one by one, for starting from the Imam down

172

to the guards and sentinels and lowest henchmen, at one time or another they had all come to her in the dark wearing a false face. But once in the House of Joy and in her bed, they took off their rubber faces and their whiskers and their beards and their turbans and their pants. So she alone of all people had seen them without their clothes, or the badges on their shoulders, or the stars on their breasts, or the medals pinned to their coats, and they all looked the same, and smelt the same, and made the same movements, for it was always they who made the movements, attacking suddenly or retreating suddenly, or raising the flag of defeat suddenly and letting it fly like a cockscomb while the rockets continued to explode in the sky and the acclamations of the people continued to resound everywhere. And she would stand half-naked under the lights, wearing her dancing costume with the brass discs snapping between her fingers, and her body hot under the sun embracing her mind, cool as the edge of a sword, and her eyes wide open and burning red, like the sun disc on a hot summer's day, and she stared into their faces one by one as they lowered their eyes to the ground, knowing that every one of them had two faces, a gentle handsome face with tears flowing from the eyes and another face dark as the devil with round bulging eyes and a nose sharp-pointed as a sword.

Her voice when she sang was music, and her body slender as a deer was love. She did not care if the stab came from behind or in front for she continued to dance. She was not worried by the thought of death, and she was not a member of Hizb Allah or Hizb Al Shaitan and she was not a man or a woman, and she was not a human being or a devil, but she was all these things at once and even if part of her happened to fall off, the whole was always there to continue the dance.

The Trial

While they were trying to pull out her head from her body they discovered that her roots were plunged deep into the soil and they became as afraid as they were tired, so they hid their fear behind their exhaustion and sat down in the shade to protect their heads from the sun. They wiped the sweat on their faces with their handkerchiefs and from under the cloth their faces were featureless as though everything had been wiped away before, leaving no trace of anything which could distinguish one face from the other, or distinguish one person from the other except a badge on the head or on the shoulder.

She managed to recognize the shoulder of the Chief of Security as he stood in front of her wiping his face with his handkerchief. He said to her: Have you got anything to say before we execute the order? What order? she asked. The order willed by the Imam, the nation and God, he said. She remained silent, not troubling to answer his question. Do you not believe in the Imam, in the nation and in God? he asked. All three of them at once? she asked. Yes, he said, either belief in all or in nothing. And again she was silent, not deigning to answer his question. He wrote something down in the book with a pen. Silence means that she is thinking and thinking indicates a lack of faith. He wiped his face with his handkerchief again and asked: Do you have anything else to say?

I want to say that I am innocent and have committed no sin and that I have one mother and she is the sun and innumerable fathers whose faces and names I do not know. I also do not read the letters of words written on paper and I live in the House of Joy but in my heart there is sadness. What is day for you is night for me and what is happiness for you is sadness for me. Pleasure for you is pain to me and victory for you means defeat to me. Your Paradise is my hell and your honour is my shame, whereas my shame is to you an honour. My reason is madness to you and my madness becomes reason for you. If my body dies my heart will live but the last thing to die in me is my mind, for it can live on the barest minimum and everything in me dies before my mind. No one of you has ever possessed my mind. No one. And no matter how often you took my body my mind was always far away out of your reach, like the eye of the sun during the day, like the eye of the sky at night.

She saw them standing in front of her in a long line, striking one palm against the other in great surprise. They said: She is neither a sorceress nor is she mad. They said: She is in complete control of her mind and what she says is reason itself. And her reason to them became more dangerous than any of her madness and they decided to condemn her to death by a method that was more rapid than stoning to death so that she would not have the opportunity to say anything further. They also decreed that her trial should not be published in the newspapers and that her file should be definitely closed and buried deep down in the earth forever.

NAWAL EL SAADAWI

She Has No Place In Paradise

A groom is filled with dread at his approaching wedding ceremony in which his manhood will be tested; his fear of his mother turns to fear and hatred for the young unknown bride he is obliged to marry. This story of power and impotence is the first in a new collection which brilliantly exposes the relationships between individuals in today's society. A man is terrified to speak the truth to men more powerfully placed than he; a woman knows nothing of the feelings her well-bred husband's friend has for her; discovering her emerging sexuality a teenager battles with her adoration and fear of her father; a worker, when tortured for information, triumphantly discovers that the essential core of himself can withdraw and survive . . .

Written by one of Egypt's leading writers, this latest volume of subtle, sharp stories on sexual politics follows Nawal El Saadawi's excellent earlier volume, *Death of an Ex-Minister*.

NAWAL EL SAADAWI

Death of An Ex-Minister

In his mother's arms, a government minister describes an encounter with a junior employee, a woman, who would not lower her eyes in his presence, would not submit. This incident, which shatters his preconceived notions of acceptable behaviour, ultimately leads to his breakdown, dismissal and death.

This cunning tale of how fear of authority, instilled in childhood, becomes authority over those perceived to be weaker – men over women – and blind subservience towards those perceived to be stronger is the first in this subtle collection by Egypt's leading female writer. While writing of Arab society, her themes are universal – the meaning of life and love in *A Modern Love Letter*; female sexuality in *The Veil*; repressed emotions in *Male Confession*.

Nawal El Saadawi's sympathetic and powerful stories of sexual politics in today's society offer a fresh and moving perception that will touch many readers.

'Nicely judged and chilling in their matter-of-factness'   CITY LIMITS
'Highly tuned political instincts ... fascinating characters'   GUARDIAN
'Powerful stories that are written simply and directly, making them all the more poignant and startling'
                                        WOMEN'S REVIEW
'They're brilliant . . . The writing is subtle and sensitive and the translation is excellent.'
                                        PUBLISHING NEWS
'A collection of remarkably controlled, provocative and well-written stories'   VENUE

MICHELLE CLIFF

No Telephone to Heaven

'One of the finest and most moving novels of the past year. In this tale of identity and nation-hood Cliff evokes a Jamaica full of contradiction and complexity, a country where history and politics are played out in surroundings of overwhelming physical beauty. Slowly the Jamaican diaspora is revealed through the novel's main character, Claire Savage, whose family emigrates to the US when she is twelve . . .

'Clare's emotional and physical journey back to Jamaica and a positive identification of herself as Jamaican takes the form of a fascinating voyage through the polarities and dualities of race and sexuality, the relationships between the first and third worlds and slavery and modern patterns of emigration. Cliff powerfully evokes the historical myths and truths of Jamaican and Black Americans, and the beauty and anguish of modern Jamaica.'

CITY LIMITS

'Michelle Cliff is a remarkable author' GUARDIAN
'Vividly and passionately written'

FINANCIAL TIMES

'The beauty and authority of her writing is coupled in a rare way with profound insight . . . it is a deeply attractive work. Full of razors and blossoms and clarity' TONI MORRISON
'A novel of great beauty' MARXISM TODAY

A Selected List of Titles Available from Minerva

Fiction

☐ 7493 9026 3	**I Pass Like Night**	Jonathan Ames	£3.99 BX
☐ 7493 9006 9	**The Tidewater Tales**	John Bath	£4.99 BX
☐ 7493 9004 2	**A Casual Brutality**	Neil Blessondath	£4.50 BX
☐ 7493 9028 2	**Interior**	Justin Cartwright	£3.99 BC
☐ 7493 9002 6	**No Telephone to Heaven**	Michelle Cliff	£3.99 BX
☐ 7493 9028 X	**Not Not While the Giro**	James Kelman	£4.50 BX
☐ 7493 9011 5	**Parable of the Blind**	Gert Hofmann	£3.99 BC
☐ 7493 9010 7	**The Inventor**	Jakov Lind	£3.99 BC
☐ 7493 9003 4	**Fall of the Imam**	Nawal El Saadewi	£3.99 BC

Non-Fiction

☐ 7493 9012 3	**Days in the Life**	Jonathon Green	£4.99 BC
☐ 7493 9019 0	**In Search of J D Salinger**	Ian Hamilton	£4.99 BX
☐ 7493 9023 9	**Stealing from a Deep Place**	Brian Hall	£3.99 BX
☐ 7493 9005 0	**The Orton Diaries**	John Lahr	£5.99 BC
☐ 7493 9014 X	**Nora**	Brenda Maddox	£6.99 BC